Warning disclaimer The following book is for entertainment and informational purposes only. The information presented is without contract or any type of guarantee assurance. While every caution has been taken to provide accurate and current information, it is solely the reader's responsibility to check all information contained in this article before relying upon it. Neither the author nor publisher can be held accountable for any errors or omissions. Under no circumstances will any legal responsibility or blame be held against the author or publisher for any reparation, damages, or monetary loss due to the information presented, either directly or indirectly. This book is not intended as legal or medical advice. If any such specialized advice is needed, seek a qualified individual for help.

Trademarks are used without permission. Use of the trademark is not authorized by, associated with, or sponsored by the trademark owners. All trademarks and brands used within this book are used with no intent to infringe on the trademark owners and only used for clarifying purposes.

Contents

SLOW COOKER PULLED PORK

Servings: 8 | Prep: 10m | Cooks: 7h | Total: 7h10m

NUTRITION FACTS

Calories: 335 | Carbohydrates: 49.4g | Fat: 5g | Protein: 21.2g | Cholesterol: 49mg

INGREDIENTS

- 1 (2 pound) pork tenderloin
- 1 (12 fluid ounce) can or bottle root beer
- 1 (18 ounce) bottle your favorite barbecue sauce
- 8 hamburger buns, split and lightly toasted

DIRECTIONS

1. Place the pork tenderloin in a slow cooker; pour the root beer over the meat. Cover and cook on low until well cooked and the pork shreds easily, 6 to 7 hours. Note: the actual length of time may vary according to individual slow cooker. Drain well. Stir in barbecue sauce. Serve over hamburger buns.

WINE BAKED POTATO

Servings: 1 | Prep: 10m | Cooks: 1h | Total: 1h10m

NUTRITION FACTS

Calories: 251 | Carbohydrates: 51.2g | Fat: 1.3g | Protein: 5g | Cholesterol: 3mg

INGREDIENTS

- 1 medium baking potato
- 1/2 medium onion, sliced
- 1/4 teaspoon butter
- 1/4 cup cooking sherry

DIRECTIONS

1. Preheat the oven to 450 degrees F (230 degrees C).
2. Make several cuts crosswise across the potato, about 1/2 inch apart and not quite all the way through. Placc half of an onion slice, and a piece of butter into each cut. Place the potato onto a sheet of aluminum foil, and form a bowl. Pour the cooking wine over the potato, and fold the foil around to seal, turning the ends up like a boat to keep the wine from spilling out.

3. Place the potato onto a baking sheet, and bake for 50 to 60 minutes, depending on the size of the potato. When done, cut through foil, and top with your favorite potato toppings or just salt and pepper.

PENNE WITH CHICKEN AND ASPARAGUS

Servings: 8 | Prep: 15m | Cooks: 20m | Total: 35m

NUTRITION FACTS

Calories: 332 | Carbohydrates: 43.3g | Fat: 10.9g | Protein: 16.7g | Cholesterol: 20mg

INGREDIENTS

- 1 (16 ounce) package dried penne pasta
- 5 tablespoons olive oil, divided
- 2 skinless, boneless chicken breast halves cut into cubes
- salt and pepper to taste
- garlic powder to taste
- 1/2 cup low-sodium chicken broth
- 1 bunch slender asparagus spears, trimmed, cut on diagonal into 1-inch pieces
- 1 clove garlic, thinly sliced
- 1/4 cup Parmesan cheese

DIRECTIONS

1. Bring a large pot of lightly salted water to boil. Add pasta, and cook until al dente, about 8 to 10 minutes. Drain, and set aside.
2. Warm 3 tablespoons olive oil in a large skillet over medium-high heat. Stir in chicken, and season with salt, pepper, and garlic powder. Cook until chicken is cooked through and browned, about 5 minutes. Remove chicken to paper towels.
3. Pour chicken broth into the skillet. Then stir in asparagus, garlic, and a pinch more garlic powder, salt, and pepper. Cover, and steam until the asparagus is just tender, about 5 to 10 minutes. Return chicken to the skillet, and warm through.
4. Stir chicken mixture into pasta, and mix well. Let sit about 5 minutes. Drizzle with 2 tablespoons olive oil, stir again, then sprinkle with Parmesan cheese.

GRILLED CILANTRO SALMON

Servings: 6 | Prep: 15m | Cooks: 20m | Total: 45m

NUTRITION FACTS

Calories: 459 | Carbohydrates: 94.3g | Fat: 4.5g | Protein: 17g | Cholesterol: 34mg

INGREDIENTS

- 1 bunch cilantro leaves, chopped
- 2 cloves garlic, chopped
- 2 cups honey
- juice from one lime
- 4 salmon steaks
- salt and pepper to taste

DIRECTIONS

1. In a small saucepan over medium-low heat, stir together cilantro, garlic, honey, and lime juice. Heat until the honey is easily stirred, about 5 minutes. Remove from heat, and let cool slightly.
2. Place salmon steaks in a baking dish, and season with salt and pepper. Pour marinade over salmon, cover, and refrigerate 10 minutes.
3. Preheat an outdoor grill for high heat.
4. Lightly oil grill grate. Place salmon steaks on grill, cook 5 minutes on each side, or until fish is easily flaked with a fork.

MARINATED BARBEQUED VEGETABLES

Servings: 5 | Prep: 20m | Cooks: 5m | Total: 1h25m | Additional: 1h

NUTRITION FACTS

Calories: 157 | Carbohydrates: 14.2g | Fat: 11.2g | Protein: 2.5g | Cholesterol: 0mg

INGREDIENTS

- 1 small eggplant, cut into 3/4 inch thick slices
- 2 small red bell peppers, seeded and cut into wide strips
- 3 zucchinis, sliced
- 6 fresh mushrooms, stems removed
- 1/4 cup olive oil
- 1/4 cup lemon juice
- 1/4 cup coarsely chopped fresh basil
- 2 cloves garlic, peeled and minced

DIRECTIONS

1. Place eggplant, red bell peppers, zucchinis and fresh mushrooms in a medium bowl.
2. In a medium bowl, whisk together olive oil, lemon juice, basil and garlic. Pour the mixture over the vegetables, cover and marinate in the refrigerator at least 1 hour.
3. Preheat an outdoor grill for high heat.
4. Place vegetables directly on the grill or on skewers. Cook on the prepared grill 2 to 3 minutes per side, brushing frequently with the marinade, or to desired doneness.

MIMI'S GIANT WHOLE-WHEAT BANANA-STRAWBERRY MUFFINS

Servings: 12 | Prep: 15m | Cooks: 20m | Total: 35m

NUTRITION FACTS

Calories: 212 | Carbohydrates: 38.1g | Fat: 5.9g | Protein: 4.2g | Cholesterol: 31mg

INGREDIENTS

- 2 eggs
- 1/2 cup unsweetened applesauce
- 1/4 cup vegetable oil
- 3/4 cup packed brown sugar
- 1 teaspoon vanilla extract
- 3 bananas, mashed
- 2 cups whole wheat flour
- 1 teaspoon baking soda
- 1 tablespoon ground cinnamon
- 1 cup frozen sliced strawberries

DIRECTIONS

1. Preheat the oven to 375 degrees F (190 degrees C). Grease 12 large muffin cups, or line with paper liners.
2. In a large bowl, whisk together the eggs, applesauce, oil, brown sugar, vanilla and bananas. Combine the flour, baking soda and cinnamon; Stir into the banana mixture until moistened. Stir in the strawberries until evenly distributed. Spoon batter into muffin cups until completely filled.
3. Bake for 20 minutes in the preheated oven, or until the tops of the muffins spring back when pressed lightly. Cool before removing from the muffin tins.

CUCUMBER-MANGO SALSA

Servings: 16 | Prep: 30m | Cooks: 2h | Total: 2h30m | Additional: 2h

NUTRITION FACTS

Calories: 32 | Carbohydrates: 8.2g | Fat: 0.1g | Protein: 0.4g | Cholesterol: 0mg

INGREDIENTS

- 3 mangos - peeled, seeded and diced
- 1 cucumber - peeled, seeded, and diced
- 2 jalapeno peppers, seeded and finely chopped
- 1 large onion, finely diced
- 1 clove garlic, minced
- 1/4 cup chopped fresh cilantro
- 1 tablespoon lime juice, or to taste
- salt and pepper to taste

DIRECTIONS

1. Stir together the mango, cucumber, jalapeno pepper, onion, garlic, and cilantro in a mixing bowl. Season with lime juice, salt, and pepper. Refrigerate at least 2 hours before serving to allow the flavors to blend.

SARAH'S APPLESAUCE

Servings: 4 | Prep: 10m | Cooks: 20m | Total: 30m

NUTRITION FACTS

Calories: 121 | Carbohydrates: 31.8g | Fat: 0.2g | Protein: 0.4g | Cholesterol: 0mg

INGREDIENTS

- 4 apples - peeled, cored and chopped
- 3/4 cup water
- 1/4 cup white sugar
- 1/2 teaspoon ground cinnamon

DIRECTIONS

1. In a saucepan, combine apples, water, sugar, and cinnamon. Cover, and cook over medium heat for 15 to 20 minutes, or until apples are soft. Allow to cool, then mash with a fork or potato masher.

REFRIED BEANS WITHOUT THE REFRY

Servings: 15 | Prep: 15m | Cooks: 8h | Total: 8h15m

NUTRITION FACTS

Calories: 139 | Carbohydrates: 25.4g | Fat: 0.5g | Protcin: 8.5g | Cholesterol: 0mg

INGREDIENTS

- 1 onion, peeled and halved
- 3 cups dry pinto beans, rinsed
- 1/2 fresh jalapeno pepper, seeded and chopped
- 2 tablespoons minced garlic
- 5 teaspoons salt
- 1 3/4 teaspoons fresh ground black pepper
- 1/8 teaspoon ground cumin, optional
- 9 cups water

DIRECTIONS

1. Place the onion, rinsed beans, jalapeno, garlic, salt, pepper, and cumin into a slow cooker. Pour in the water and stir to combine. Cook on High for 8 hours, adding more water as needed. Note: if more than 1 cup of water has evaporated during cooking, then the temperature is too high.
2. Once the beans have cooked, strain them, and reserve the liquid. Mash the beans with a potato masher, adding the reserved water as needed to attain desired consistency.

HOMEMADE BLACK BEAN VEGGIE BURGERS

Servings: 4 | Prep: 15m | Cooks: 20m | Total: 35m

NUTRITION FACTS

Calories: 198 | Carbohydrates: 33.1g | Fat: 3g | Protein: 11.2g | Cholesterol: 46mg

INGREDIENTS

- 1 (16 ounce) can black beans, drained and rinsed
- 1/2 green bell pepper, cut into 2 inch pieces
- 1/2 onion, cut into wedges
- 1 tablespoon chili powder
- 1 tablespoon cumin
- 1 teaspoon Thai chili sauce or hot sauce

- 3 cloves garlic, peeled
- 1 egg
- 1/2 cup bread crumbs

DIRECTIONS

1. If grilling, preheat an outdoor grill for high heat, and lightly oil a sheet of aluminum foil. If baking, preheat oven to 375 degrees F (190 degrees C), and lightly oil a baking sheet.
2. In a medium bowl, mash black beans with a fork until thick and pasty.
3. In a food processor, finely chop bell pepper, onion, and garlic. Then stir into mashed beans.
4. In a small bowl, stir together egg, chili powder, cumin, and chili sauce.
5. Stir the egg mixture into the mashed beans. Mix in bread crumbs until the mixture is sticky and holds together. Divide mixture into four patties.
6. If grilling, place patties on foil, and grill about 8 minutes on each side. If baking, place patties on baking sheet, and bake about 10 minutes on each side.

BEST SPANISH RICE

Servings: 5 | Prep: 10m | Cooks: 20m | Total: 30m

NUTRITION FACTS

Calories: 286 | Carbohydrates: 50.9g | Fat: 6.2g | Protein: 5.7g | Cholesterol: 2mg

INGREDIENTS

- 2 tablespoons oil
- 2 tablespoons chopped onion
- 1 1/2 cups uncooked white rice
- 2 cups chicken broth
- 1 cup chunky salsa

DIRECTIONS

1. Heat oil in a large, heavy skillet over medium heat. Stir in onion, and cook until tender, about 5 minutes.
2. Mix rice into skillet, stirring often. When rice begins to brown, stir in chicken broth and salsa. Reduce heat, cover and simmer 20 minutes, until liquid has been absorbed.

ASIAN ORANGE CHICKEN

Servings: 4 | Prep: 40m | Cooks: 40m | Total: 3h20m | Additional: 2h

NUTRITION FACTS

Calories: 445 | Carbohydrates: 68.7g | Fat: 11.2g | Protein: 17.8g | Cholesterol: 34mg

INGREDIENTS

- 1 1/2 cups water
- 2 tablespoons orange juice
- 1/4 cup lemon juice
- 1/3 cup rice vinegar
- 2 1/2 tablespoons soy sauce
- 1 tablespoon grated orange zest
- 1 cup packed brown sugar
- 1/2 teaspoon minced fresh ginger root
- 1/2 teaspoon minced garlic
- 2 tablespoons chopped green onion
- 1/4 teaspoon red pepper flakes
- 3 tablespoons cornstarch
- 2 tablespoons water
- 2 boneless, skinless chicken breasts, cut into 1/2 inch pieces
- 1 cup all-purpose flour
- 1/4 teaspoon salt
- 1/4 teaspoon pepper
- 3 tablespoons olive oil

DIRECTIONS

1. Pour 1 1/2 cups water, orange juice, lemon juice, rice vinegar, and soy sauce into a saucepan and set over medium-high heat. Stir in the orange zest, brown sugar, ginger, garlic, chopped onion, and red pepper flakes. Bring to a boil. Remove from heat, and cool 10 to 15 minutes.
2. Place the chicken pieces into a resealable plastic bag. When contents of saucepan have cooled, pour 1 cup of sauce into bag. Reserve the remaining sauce. Seal the bag, and refrigerate at least 2 hours.
3. In another resealable plastic bag, mix the flour, salt, and pepper. Add the marinated chicken pieces, seal the bag, and shake to coat.
4. Heat the olive oil in a large skillet over medium heat. Place chicken into the skillet, and brown on both sides. Drain on a plate lined with paper towels, and cover with aluminum foil.
5. Wipe out the skillet, and add the sauce. Bring to a boil over medium-high heat. Mix together the cornstarch and 2 tablespoons water; stir into the sauce. Reduce heat to medium low, add the chicken pieces, and simmer, about 5 minutes, stirring occasionally.

SPANISH RICE

Servings: 4 | Prep: 10m | Cooks: 30m | Total: 40m

NUTRITION FACTS

Calories: 270 | Carbohydrates: 45.7g | Fat: 7.6g | Protein: 4.8g | Cholesterol: 0mg

INGREDIENTS

- 2 tablespoons vegetable oil
- 1 cup uncooked white rice
- 1 onion, chopped
- 1/2 green bell pepper, chopped
- 2 cups water
- 1 (10 ounce) can diced tomatoes and green chiles
- 2 teaspoons chili powder, or to taste
- 1 teaspoon salt

DIRECTIONS

1. Heat oil in a deep skillet over medium heat. Saute rice, onion, and bell pepper until rice is browned and onions are tender.
2. Stir in water and tomatoes. Season with chili powder and salt. Cover, and simmer for 30 minutes, or until rice is cooked and liquid is absorbed.

OVEN ROASTED POTATOES

Servings: 4 | Prep: 15m | Cooks: 30m | Total: 45m

NUTRITION FACTS

Calories: 289 | Carbohydrates: 53.1g | Fat: 7.1g | Protein: 5g | Cholesterol: 0mg

INGREDIENTS

- 1/8 cup olive oil
- 1 tablespoon minced garlic
- 1/2 teaspoon dried basil
- 1/2 teaspoon dried marjoram
- 1/2 teaspoon dried dill weed
- 1/2 teaspoon dried oregano
- 1/2 teaspoon dried parsley
- 1/2 teaspoon crushed red pepper flakes
- 1/2 teaspoon salt
- 4 large potatoes, peeled and cubed

- 1/2 teaspoon dried thyme

DIRECTIONS

1. Preheat oven to 475 degrees F (245 degrees C).
2. In a large bowl, combine oil, garlic, basil, marjoram, dill weed, thyme, oregano, parsley, red pepper flakes, and salt. Stir in potatoes until evenly coated. Place potatoes in a single layer on a roasting pan or baking sheet.
3. Roast for 20 to 30 minutes in the preheated oven, turning occasionally to brown on all sides.

PRETZEL TURTLES

Servings: 20 | Prep: 10m | Cooks: 4m | Total: 14m

NUTRITION FACTS

Calories: 82 | Carbohydrates: 14.1g | Fat: 2.2g | Protein: 1.7g | Cholesterol: 1mg

INGREDIENTS

- 20 small mini pretzels
- 20 chocolate covered caramel candies
- 20 pecan halves
-

DIRECTIONS

1. Preheat oven to 300 degrees F (150 degrees C).
2. Arrange the pretzels in a single layer on a parchment lined cookie sheet. Place one chocolate covered caramel candy on each pretzel.
3. Bake for 4 minutes. While the candy is warm, press a pecan half onto each candy covered pretzel. Cool completely before storing in an airtight container.

FRIED RICE RESTAURANT STYLE

Servings: 8 | Prep: 15m | Cooks: 30m | Total: 45m

NUTRITION FACTS

Calories: 261 | Carbohydrates: 39.7g | Fat: 8.4g | Protein: 5.8g | Cholesterol: 46mg

INGREDIENTS

- 2 cups enriched white rice
- 4 cups water
- 2/3 cup chopped baby carrots
- 1/2 cup frozen green peas
- 2 tablespoons vegetable oil
- 2 eggs
- soy sauce to taste
- sesame oil, to taste (optional)

DIRECTIONS

1. In a saucepan, combine rice and water. Bring to a boil. Reduce heat, cover, and simmer for 20 minutes.
2. In a small saucepan, boil carrots in water about 3 to 5 minutes. Drop peas into boiling water, and drain.
3. Heat wok over high heat. Pour in oil, then stir in carrots and peas; cook about 30 seconds. Crack in eggs, stirring quickly to scramble eggs with vegetables. Stir in cooked rice. Shake in soy sauce, and toss rice to coat. Drizzle with sesame oil, and toss again.

DUMPLINGS

Servings: 6 | Prep: 5m | Cooks: 15m | Total: 20m

NUTRITION FACTS

Calories: 105 | Carbohydrates: 18g | Fat: 2.4g | Protein: 2.8g | Cholesterol: 2mg

INGREDIENTS

- 1 cup all-purpose flour
- 2 teaspoons baking powder
- 1 teaspoon white sugar
- 1/2 teaspoon salt
- 1 tablespoon margarine
- 1/2 cup milk

DIRECTIONS

1. Stir together flour, baking powder, sugar, and salt in medium size bowl. Cut in butter until crumbly. Stir in milk to make a soft dough.
2. Drop by spoonfuls into boiling stew. Cover and simmer 15 minutes without lifting lid. Serve.
3. To make parsley dumplings, add 1 tablespoon parsley flakes to the dry ingredients.

RED LENTIL CURRY

Servings: 8 | Prep: 10m | Cooks: 30m | Total: 40m

NUTRITION FACTS

Calories: 192 | Carbohydrates: 32.5g | Fat: 2.6g | Protein: 12.1g | Cholesterol: 0mg

INGREDIENTS

- 2 cups red lentils
- 1 large onion, diced
- 1 tablespoon vegetable oil
- 2 tablespoons curry paste
- 1 tablespoon curry powder
- 1 teaspoon ground turmeric
- 1 teaspoon ground cumin
- 1 teaspoon chili powder
- 1 teaspoon salt
- 1 teaspoon white sugar
- 1 teaspoon minced garlic
- 1 teaspoon minced fresh ginger
- 1 (14.25 ounce) can tomato puree

DIRECTIONS

1. Wash the lentils in cold water until the water runs clear. Put lentils in a pot with enough water to cover; bring to a boil, place a cover on the pot, reduce heat to medium-low, and simmer, adding water during cooking as needed to keep covered, until tender, 15 to 20 minutes. Drain.
2. Heat vegetable oil in a large skillet over medium heat; cook and stir onions in hot oil until caramelized, about 20 minutes.
3. Mix curry paste, curry powder, turmeric, cumin, chili powder, salt, sugar, garlic, and ginger together in a large bowl; stir into the onions. Increase heat to high and cook, stirring constantly, until fragrant, 1 to 2 minutes.
4. Stir in the tomato puree, remove from heat and stir into the lentils.

BOSTON BAKED BEANS

Servings: 6 | Prep: 30m | Cooks: 4h | Total: 5h | Additional: 30m

NUTRITION FACTS

Calories: 382 | Carbohydrates: 63.1g | Fat: 6.3g | Protein: 20.7g | Cholesterol: 14mg

INGREDIENTS

- 2 cups navy beans
- 1/4 teaspoon ground black pepper

- 1/2 pound bacon
- 1 onion, finely diced
- 3 tablespoons molasses
- 2 teaspoons salt
- 1/4 teaspoon dry mustard
- 1/2 cup ketchup
- 1 tablespoon Worcestershire sauce
- 1/4 cup brown sugar

DIRECTIONS

1. Soak beans overnight in cold water. Simmer the beans in the same water until tender, approximately 1 to 2 hours. Drain and reserve the liquid.
2. Preheat oven to 325 degrees F (165 degrees C).
3. Arrange the beans in a 2 quart bean pot or casserole dish by placing a portion of the beans in the bottom of dish, and layering them with bacon and onion.
4. In a saucepan, combine molasses, salt, pepper, dry mustard, ketchup, Worcestershire sauce and brown sugar. Bring the mixture to a boil and pour over beans. Pour in just enough of the reserved bean water to cover the beans. Cover the dish with a lid or aluminum foil.
5. Bake for 3 to 4 hours in the preheated oven, until beans are tender. Remove the lid about halfway through cooking, and add more liquid if necessary to prevent the beans from getting too dry.

BLACK BEANS AND RICE

Servings: 10 | Prep: 5m | Cooks: 25m | Total: 30m

NUTRITION FACTS

Calories: 140 | Carbohydrates: 27.1g | Fat: 0.9g | Protein: 6.3g | Cholesterol: 0mg

INGREDIENTS

- 1 teaspoon olive oil
- 1 onion, chopped
- 2 cloves garlic, minced
- 3/4 cup uncooked white rice
- 1 1/2 cups low sodium, low fat vegetable broth
- 1 teaspoon ground cumin
- 1/4 teaspoon cayenne pepper
- 3 1/2 cups canned black beans, drained

DIRECTIONS

1. In a stockpot over medium-high heat, heat the oil. Add the onion and garlic and saute for 4 minutes. Add the rice and saute for 2 minutes.
2. Add the vegetable broth, bring to a boil, cover and lower the heat and cook for 20 minutes. Add the spices and black beans.

MEXICAN RICE

Servings: 6 | Prep: 5m | Cooks: 25m | Total: 30m

NUTRITION FACTS

Calories: 158 | Carbohydrates: 29.1g | Fat: 2.8g | Protein: 3.4g | Cholesterol: 1mg

INGREDIENTS

- 1 cup long grain white rice
- 1 tablespoon vegetable oil
- 1 1/2 cups chicken broth
- 1/2 onion, finely chopped
- 1/2 green bell pepper, finely chopped
- 1 fresh jalapeno pepper, chopped
- 1 tomato, seeded and chopped
- 1 cube chicken bouillon
- salt and pepper to taste
- 1/2 teaspoon ground cumin
- 1/2 cup chopped fresh cilantro
- 1 clove garlic, halved

DIRECTIONS

1. In a medium sauce pan, cook rice in oil over medium heat for about 3 minutes. Pour in chicken broth, and bring to a boil. Stir in onion, green pepper, jalapeno, and diced tomato. Season with bouillon cube, salt and pepper, cumin, cilantro, and garlic. Bring to a boil, cover, and reduce heat to low. Cook for 20 minutes.

BROCCOLI BEEF

Servings: 4 | Prep: 15m | Cooks: 15m | Total: 30m

NUTRITION FACTS

Calories: 178 | Carbohydrates: 19g | Fat: 3.2g | Protein: 19.2g | Cholesterol: 39mg

INGREDIENTS

- 1/4 cup all-purpose flour
- 1 (10.5 ounce) can beef broth
- 2 tablespoons white sugar
- 2 tablespoons soy sauce
- 1 pound boneless round steak, cut into bite size pieces
- 1/4 teaspoon chopped fresh ginger root
- 1 clove garlic, minced
- 4 cups chopped fresh broccoli

DIRECTIONS

1. In a small bowl, combine flour, broth, sugar, and soy sauce. Stir until sugar and flour are dissolved.
2. In a large skillet or wok over high heat, cook and stir beef 2 to 4 minutes, or until browned. Stir in broth mixture, ginger, garlic, and broccoli. Bring to a boil, then reduce heat. Simmer 5 to 10 minutes, or until sauce thickens.

PESTO PASTA WITH CHICKEN

Servings: 8 | Prep: 10m | Cooks: 20m | Total: 30m

NUTRITION FACTS

Calories: 328 | Carbohydrates: 43.3g | Fat: 10.1g | Protein: 17.4g | Cholesterol: 22mg

INGREDIENTS

- 1 (16 ounce) package bow tie pasta
- 1 teaspoon olive oil
- 2 cloves garlic, minced
- 2 boneless skinless chicken breasts, cut into bite-size pieces
- crushed red pepper flakes to taste
- 1/3 cup oil-packed sun-dried tomatoes, drained and cut into strips
- 1/2 cup pesto sauce

DIRECTIONS

1. Bring a large pot of lightly salted water to a boil. Add pasta and cook for 8 to 10 minutes or until al dente; drain.

2. Heat oil in a large skillet over medium heat. Saute garlic until tender, then stir in chicken. Season with red pepper flakes. Cook until chicken is golden, and cooked through.
3. In a large bowl, combine pasta, chicken, sun-dried tomatoes and pesto. Toss to coat evenly.

MONGOLIAN BEEF AND SPRING ONIONS

Servings: 4 | Prep: 12m | Cooks: 8m | Total: 30m | Additional: 10m

NUTRITION FACTS

Calories: 391 | Carbohydrates: 54.7g | Fat: 12.1g | Protein: 18g | Cholesterol: 27mg

INGREDIENTS

- 2 teaspoons vegetable oil
- 1 tablespoon finely chopped garlic
- 1/2 teaspoon grated fresh ginger root
- 1/2 cup soy sauce
- 1/2 cup water
- 2/3 cup dark brown sugar
- 1 pound beef flank steak, sliced 1/4 inch thick on the diagonal
- 1/4 cup cornstarch
- 1 cup vegetable oil for frying
- 2 bunches green onions, cut in 2-inch lengths

DIRECTIONS

1. Heat 2 teaspoons of vegetable oil in a saucepan over medium heat, and cook and stir the garlic and ginger until they release their fragrance, about 30 seconds. Pour in the soy sauce, water, and brown sugar. Raise the heat to medium-high, and stir 4 minutes, until the sugar has dissolved and the sauce boils and slightly thickens. Remove sauce from the heat, and set aside.
2. Place the sliced beef into a bowl, and stir the cornstarch into the beef, coating it thoroughly. Allow the beef and cornstarch to sit until most of the juices from the meat have been absorbed by the cornstarch, about 10 minutes.
3. Heat the vegetable oil in a deep-sided skillet or wok to 375 degrees F (190 degrees C).
4. Shake excess cornstarch from the beef slices, and drop them into the hot oil, a few at a time. Stir briefly, and fry until the edges become crisp and start to brown, about 2 minutes. Remove the beef from the oil with a large slotted spoon, and allow to drain on paper towels to remove excess oil.
5. Pour the oil out of the skillet or wok, and return the pan to medium heat. Return the beef slices to the pan, stir briefly, and pour in the reserved sauce. Stir once or twice to combine, and add the green onions. Bring the mixture to a boil, and cook until the onions have softened and turned bright green, about 2 minutes.

SWEET POTATO CASSEROLE

Servings: 8 | Prep: 15m | Cooks: 45m | Total: 1h

NUTRITION FACTS

Calories: 267 | Carbohydrates: 60.4g | Fat: 2.6g | Protein: 2g | Cholesterol: 0mg

INGREDIENTS

- 5 sweet potatoes, sliced
- 1/4 cup reduced fat margarine
- 1/2 cup packed brown sugar
- 3 tablespoons orange juice
- 1 pinch ground cinnamon
- 1 (10.5 ounce) package miniature marshmallows

DIRECTIONS

1. Preheat oven to 350 degrees F (175 degrees C).
2. Place sweet potatoes in a large saucepan with enough water to cover. Bring to a boil, and cook until tender, about 15 minutes. Remove from heat, drain, and mash.
3. Place mashed sweet potatoes in large bowl, and use an electric mixer to blend with the margarine, brown sugar, orange juice, and cinnamon. Spread evenly into a 9x13 inch baking dish. Top with miniature marshmallows.
4. Bake for 25 to 30 minutes in the preheated oven, or until heated through, and marshmallows are puffed and golden brown.

SALSA CHICKEN BURRITO FILLING

Servings: 4 | Prep: 5m | Cooks: 30m | Total: 35m

NUTRITION FACTS

Calories: 107 | Carbohydrates: 9.6g | Fat: 1.5g | Protein: 12.3g | Cholesterol: 30mg

INGREDIENTS

- 2 skinless, boneless chicken breast halves
- 1 (4 ounce) can tomato sauce
- 1/4 cup salsa
- 1 (1.25 ounce) package taco seasoning mix
- 1 teaspoon ground cumin
- 2 cloves garlic, minced
- 1 teaspoon chili powder
- hot sauce to taste

DIRECTIONS

1. Place chicken breasts and tomato sauce in a medium saucepan over medium high heat. Bring to a boil, then add the salsa, seasoning, cumin, garlic and chili powder. Let simmer for 15 minutes.
2. With a fork, start pulling the chicken meat apart into thin strings. Keep cooking pulled chicken meat and sauce, covered, for another 5 to 10 minutes. Add hot sauce to taste and stir together (Note: You may need to add a bit of water if the mixture is cooked too high and gets too thick.)

GARLIC CHICKEN WITH ORZO NOODLES

Servings: 4 | Prep: 15m | Cooks: 15m | Total: 30m

NUTRITION FACTS

Calories: 351 | Carbohydrates: 40.4g | Fat: 10.6g | Protein: 22.3g | Cholesterol: 38mg

INGREDIENTS

- 1 cup uncooked orzo pasta
- 2 tablespoons olive oil
- 2 cloves garlic
- 1/4 teaspoon crushed red pepper
- 2 skinless, boneless chicken breast halves - cut into bite-size pieces
- salt to taste
- 1 tablespoon chopped fresh parsley
- 2 cups fresh spinach leaves
- grated Parmesan cheese for topping

DIRECTIONS

1. Bring a large pot of lightly salted water to a boil. Add orzo pasta, cook for 8 to 10 minutes, until al dente, and drain.
2. Heat the oil in a skillet over medium-high heat, and cook the garlic and red pepper 1 minute, until garlic is golden brown. Stir in chicken, season with salt, and cook 2 to 5 minutes, until lightly browned and juices run clear. Reduce heat to medium, and mix in the parsley and cooked orzo. Place spinach in the skillet. Continue cooking 5 minutes, stirring occasionally, until spinach is wilted. Serve topped with Parmesan cheese.

HOMEMADE CRISPY SEASONED FRENCH FRIES

Servings: 8 | Prep: 15m | Cooks: 10m | Total: 25m

NUTRITION FACTS

Calories: 192 | Carbohydrates: 37.8g | Fat: 3.1g | Protein: 3.9g | Cholesterol: 0mg

INGREDIENTS

- 2 1/2 pounds russet potatoes, peeled
- 1 cup all-purpose flour
- 1 teaspoon garlic salt
- 1 teaspoon onion salt
- 1 teaspoon salt
- 1 teaspoon paprika
- 1/2 cup water, or as needed
- 1 cup vegetable oil for frying

DIRECTIONS

1. Slice potatoes into French fries, and place into cold water so they won't turn brown while you prepare the oil.
2. Heat oil in a large skillet over medium-high heat. While the oil is heating, sift the flour, garlic salt, onion salt, (regular) salt, and paprika into a large bowl. Gradually stir in enough water so that the mixture can be drizzled from a spoon.
3. Dip potato slices into the batter one at a time, and place in the hot oil so they are not touching at first. The fries must be placed into the skillet one at a time, or they will clump together. Fry until golden brown and crispy. Remove and drain on paper towels.

TURKEY VEGGIE MEATLOAF CUPS

Servings: 10 | Prep: 20m | Cooks: 25m | Total: 50m

NUTRITION FACTS

Calories: 119 | Carbohydrates: 13.6g | Fat: 1g | Protein: 13.2g | Cholesterol: 47mg

INGREDIENTS

- 2 cups coarsely chopped zucchini
- 1 1/2 cups coarsely chopped onions
- 1 red bell pepper, coarsely chopped
- 1 egg
- 2 tablespoons Worcestershire sauce
- 1 tablespoon Dijon mustard

- 1 pound extra lean ground turkey
- 1/2 cup uncooked couscous
- 1/2 cup barbecue sauce, or as needed

DIRECTIONS

1. Preheat oven to 400 degrees F (200 degrees C). Spray 20 muffin cups with cooking spray.
2. Place zucchini, onions, and red bell pepper into a food processor, and pulse several times until finely chopped but not liquefied. Place the vegetables into a bowl, and mix in ground turkey, couscous, egg, Worcestershire sauce, and Dijon mustard until thoroughly combined. Fill each prepared muffin cup about 3/4 full. Top each cup with about 1 teaspoon of barbecue sauce.
3. Bake in the preheated oven until juices run clear, about 25 minutes. Internal temperature of a muffin measured by an instant-read meat thermometer should be at least 160 degrees F (70 degrees C). Let stand 5 minutes before serving.

PAT'S BAKED BEANS

Servings: 10 | Prep: 15m | Cooks: 1h15m | Total: 1h30m

NUTRITION FACTS

Calories: 399 | Carbohydrates: 68g | Fat: 9.1g | Protein: 14.1g | Cholesterol: 12mg

INGREDIENTS

- 6 slices bacon
- 1 cup chopped onion
- 1 clove garlic, minced
- 1 (16 ounce) can pinto beans
- 1 (16 ounce) can great Northern beans, drained
- 1 (16 ounce) can baked beans
- 1 (16 ounce) can red kidney beans, drained
- 1 (15 ounce) can garbanzo beans, drained
- 3/4 cup ketchup
- 1/2 cup molasses
- 1/4 cup packed brown sugar
- 2 tablespoons Worcestershire sauce
- 1 tablespoon yellow mustard
- 1/2 teaspoon pepper

DIRECTIONS

1. Preheat oven to 375 degrees F (190 degrees C).

2. Place bacon in a large, deep skillet. Cook over medium high heat until evenly brown. Drain, reserving 2 tablespoons of drippings, crumble and set aside in a large bowl. Cook the onion and garlic in the reserved drippings until onion is tender; drain excess grease and transfer to the bowl with the bacon.
3. To the bacon and onions add pinto beans, northern beans, baked beans, kidney beans and garbanzo beans. Stir in ketchup, molasses, brown sugar, Worcestershire sauce, mustard and black pepper. Mix well and transfer to a 9x12 inch casserole dish.
4. Cover and bake in preheated oven for 1 hour.

BEST BLACK BEANS

Servings: 4 | Prep: 10m | Cooks: 5m | Total: 15m

NUTRITION FACTS

Calories: 112 | Carbohydrates: 20.8g | Fat: 0.4g | Protein: 7.1g | Cholesterol: 0mg

INGREDIENTS

- 1 (16 ounce) can black beans
- 1 small onion, chopped
- 1 clove garlic, chopped
- 1 tablespoon chopped fresh cilantro
- 1/4 teaspoon cayenne pepper
- salt to taste

DIRECTIONS

1. In a medium saucepan, combine beans, onion, and garlic, and bring to a boil. Reduce heat to medium-low. Season with cilantro, cayenne, and salt. Simmer for 5 minutes, and serve.

QUICK BAKED ZUCCHINI CHIPS

Servings: 4 | Prep: 5m | Cooks: 10m | Total: 15m

NUTRITION FACTS

Calories: 92 | Carbohydrates: 13.8g | Fat: 1.7g | Protein: 6.1g | Cholesterol: 2mg

INGREDIENTS

- 2 medium zucchini, cut into 1/4-inch slices
- 1/2 cup seasoned dry bread crumbs
- 2 tablespoons grated Parmesan cheese
- 2 egg whites

- 1/8 teaspoon ground black pepper

DIRECTIONS

1. Preheat the oven to 475 degrees F (245 degrees C).
2. In one small bowl, stir together the bread crumbs, pepper and Parmesan cheese. Place the egg whites in a separate bowl. Dip zucchini slices into the egg whites, then coat the breadcrumb mixture. Place on a greased baking sheet.
3. Bake for 5 minutes in the preheated oven, then turn over and bake for another 5 to 10 minutes, until browned and crispy.

SLOW COOKER SPICY BLACK-EYED PEAS

Servings: 10 | Prep: 30m | Cooks: 6h | Total: 6h30m

NUTRITION FACTS

Calories: 199 | Carbohydrates: 30.2g | Fat: 2.9g | Protein: 14.1g | Cholesterol: 10mg

INGREDIENTS

- 6 cups water
- 1 cube chicken bouillon
- 1 pound dried black-eyed peas, sorted and rinsed
- 1 onion, diced
- 2 cloves garlic, diced
- 1 red bell pepper, stemmed, seeded, and diced
- 1 jalapeno chile, seeded and minced
- 8 ounces diced ham
- 4 slices bacon, chopped
- 1/2 teaspoon cayenne pepper
- 1 1/2 teaspoons cumin
- salt, to taste
- 1 teaspoon ground black pepper

DIRECTIONS

1. Pour the water into a slow cooker, add the bouillon cube, and stir to dissolve. Combine the black-eyed peas, onion, garlic, bell pepper, jalapeno pepper, ham, bacon, cayenne pepper, cumin, salt, and pepper; stir to blend. Cover the slow cooker and cook on Low for 6 to 8 hours until the beans are tender.

CARROT RICE

Servings: 6 | Prep: 15m | Cooks: 20m | Total: 35m

NUTRITION FACTS

Calories: 179 | Carbohydrates: 30.1g | Fat: 4.8g | Protein: 4g | Cholesterol: 0mg

INGREDIENTS

- 1 cup basmati rice
- 2 cups water
- 1/4 cup roasted peanuts
- 1 tablespoon margarine
- 1 onion, sliced
- 1 teaspoon minced fresh ginger root
- 3/4 cup grated carrots
- salt to taste
- cayenne pepper to taste
- chopped fresh cilantro

DIRECTIONS

1. Combine rice and water in a medium saucepan. Bring to a boil over high heat. Reduce heat to low, cover with lid, and allow to steam until tender, about 20 minutes.
2. While rice is cooking, grind peanuts in a blender and set aside. Heat the margarine in a skillet over medium heat. Stir in the onion; cook and stir until the onion has softened and turned golden brown about 10 minutes. Stir in ginger, carrots, and salt to taste. Reduce heat to low and cover to steam 5 minutes. Stir in cayenne pepper and peanuts. When rice is done, add it to skillet and stir gently to combine with other ingredients. Garnish with chopped cilantro.

ROASTED BEETS 'N' SWEETS

Servings: 6 | Prep: 15m | Cooks: 1h | Total: 1h15m

NUTRITION FACTS

Calories: 198 | Carbohydrates: 34.3g | Fat: 5.9g | Protein: 3.5g | Cholesterol: 0mg

INGREDIENTS

- 6 medium beets, peeled and cut into chunks
- 2 1/2 tablespoons olive oil, divided
- 1 teaspoon ground black pepper
- 1 teaspoon sugar

- 1 teaspoon garlic powder
- 1 teaspoon kosher salt
- 3 medium sweet potatoes, cut into chunks
- 1 large sweet onion, chopped

DIRECTIONS

1. Preheat oven to 400 degrees F (200 degrees C).
2. In a bowl, toss the beets with 1/2 tablespoon olive oil to coat. Spread in a single layer on a baking sheet.
3. Mix the remaining 2 tablespoons olive oil, garlic powder, salt, pepper, and sugar in a large resealable plastic bag. Place the sweet potatoes and onion in the bag. Seal bag, and shake to coat vegetables with the oil mixture.
4. Bake beets 15 minutes in the preheated oven. Mix sweet potato mixture with the beets on the baking sheet. Continue baking 45 minutes, stirring after 20 minutes, until all vegetables are tender.

SPICED SWEET ROASTED RED PEPPER HUMMUS

Servings: 8 | Prep: 15m | Cooks: 1h | Total: 1h15m | Additional: 1h

NUTRITION FACTS

Calories: 64 | Carbohydrates: 9.6g | Fat: 2.2g | Protein: 2.5g | Cholesterol: 0mg

INGREDIENTS

- 1 (15 ounce) can garbanzo beans, drained
- 1 (4 ounce) jar roasted red peppers
- 3 tablespoons lemon juice
- 1 1/2 tablespoons tahini
- 1 clove garlic, minced
- 1/2 teaspoon ground cumin
- 1/2 teaspoon cayenne pepper
- 1/4 teaspoon salt
- 1 tablespoon chopped fresh parsley

DIRECTIONS

1. In an electric blender or food processor, puree the chickpeas, red peppers, lemon juice, tahini, garlic, cumin, cayenne, and salt. Process, using long pulses, until the mixture is fairly smooth, and slightly fluffy. Make sure to scrape the mixture off the sides of the food processor or blender in between

pulses. Transfer to a serving bowl and refrigerate for at least 1 hour. (The hummus can be made up to 3 days ahead and refrigerated. Return to room temperature before serving.)

2. Sprinkle the hummus with the chopped parsley before serving.

BAKED SWEET POTATOES

Servings: 4 | Prep: 10m | Cooks: 1h5m | Total: 1h15m

NUTRITION FACTS

Calories: 321 | Carbohydrates: 61g | Fat: 7.3g | Protein: 4.8g | Cholesterol: 0mg

INGREDIENTS

- 2 tablespoons olive oil
- 3 large sweet potatoes
- 2 pinches dried oregano
- 2 pinches salt
- 2 pinches ground black pepper

DIRECTIONS

1. Preheat oven to 350 degrees F (175 degrees C). Coat the bottom of a glass or non-stick baking dish with olive oil, just enough to coat.
2. Wash and peel the sweet potatoes. Cut them into medium size pieces. Place the cut sweet potatoes in the baking dish and turn them so that they are coated with the olive oil. Sprinkle moderately with oregano, and salt and pepper (to taste).
3. Bake in a preheated 350 degrees F (175 degrees C) oven for 60 minutes or until soft.

VIETNAMESE FRESH SPRING ROLLS

Servings: 8 | Prep: 45m | Cooks: 5m | Total: 50m

NUTRITION FACTS

Calories: 82 | Carbohydrates: 15.8g | Fat: 0.7g | Protein: 3.3g | Cholesterol: 11mg

INGREDIENTS

- 2 ounces rice vermicelli
- 8 rice wrappers (8.5 inch diameter)
- 1/4 cup water
- 2 tablespoons fresh lime juice

- 8 large cooked shrimp - peeled, deveined and cut in half
- 1 1/3 tablespoons chopped fresh Thai basil
- 3 tablespoons chopped fresh mint leaves
- 3 tablespoons chopped fresh cilantro
- 2 leaves lettuce, chopped
- 4 teaspoons fish sauce
- 1 clove garlic, minced
- 2 tablespoons white sugar
- 1/2 teaspoon garlic chili sauce
- 3 tablespoons hoisin sauce
- 1 teaspoon finely chopped peanuts

DIRECTIONS

1. Bring a medium saucepan of water to boil. Boil rice vermicelli 3 to 5 minutes, or until al dente, and drain.
2. Fill a large bowl with warm water. Dip one wrapper into the hot water for 1 second to soften. Lay wrapper flat. In a row across the center, place 2 shrimp halves, a handful of vermicelli, basil, mint, cilantro and lettuce, leaving about 2 inches uncovered on each side. Fold uncovered sides inward, then tightly roll the wrapper, beginning at the end with the lettuce. Repeat with remaining ingredients.
3. In a small bowl, mix the fish sauce, water, lime juice, garlic, sugar and chili sauce.
4. In another small bowl, mix the hoisin sauce and peanuts.
5. Serve rolled spring rolls with the fish sauce and hoisin sauce mixtures.

CHICKPEA CURRY

Servings: 8 | Prep: 10m | Cooks: 30m | Total: 40m

NUTRITION FACTS

Calories: 135 | Carbohydrates: 20.5g | Fat: 4.5g | Protein: 4.1g | Cholesterol: 0mg

INGREDIENTS

- 2 tablespoons vegetable oil
- 2 onions, minced
- 2 cloves garlic, minced
- 2 teaspoons fresh ginger root, finely chopped
- 1 teaspoon ground coriander
- salt
- 1 teaspoon cayenne pepper
- 1 teaspoon ground turmeric

- 6 whole cloves
- 2 (2 inch) sticks cinnamon, crushed
- 1 teaspoon ground cumin
- 2 (15 ounce) cans garbanzo beans
- 1 cup chopped fresh cilantro

DIRECTIONS

1. Heat oil in a large frying pan over medium heat, and fry onions until tender.
2. Stir in garlic, ginger, cloves, cinnamon, cumin, coriander, salt, cayenne, and turmeric. Cook for 1 minute over medium heat, stirring constantly. Mix in garbanzo beans and their liquid. Continue to cook and stir until all ingredients are well blended and heated through. Remove from heat. Stir in cilantro just before serving, reserving 1 tablespoon for garnish.

ROAST POTATOES

Servings: 4 | Prep: 10m | Cooks: 20m | Total: 30m

NUTRITION FACTS

Calories: 227 | Carbohydrates: 36.4g | Fat: 7.3g | Protein: 4.3g | Cholesterol: 0mg

INGREDIENTS

- 2 pounds red potatoes, cut into quarters
- 2 tablespoons vegetable oil
- 1 teaspoon salt
- 1/2 teaspoon freshly ground black pepper
- 1/2 teaspoon dried rosemary, crushed

DIRECTIONS

1. Preheat oven to 450 degrees F (250 degrees C).
2. Place potatoes in a large roasting pan and toss with oil, salt, pepper, and rosemary until evenly coated. Spread out potatoes in a single layer.
3. Bake in preheated oven for 20 minutes, stirring occasionally. Serve immediately.

BAKED BEANS

Servings: 6 | Prep: 20m | Cooks: 1h | Total: 1h20m

NUTRITION FACTS

Calories: 287 | Carbohydrates: 52.3g | Fat: 6.5g | Protein: 8.9g | Cholesterol: 16mg

INGREDIENTS

- 2 (15 ounce) cans baked beans with pork
- 1/2 cup packed brown sugar
- 1/2 onion, chopped
- 1/2 cup ketchup
- 1 tablespoon prepared mustard
- 1 teaspoon Worcestershire sauce
- 1 teaspoon red wine vinegar
- salt and pepper to taste
- 2 slices bacon

DIRECTIONS

1. Preheat oven to 350 degrees F (175 degrees C).
2. In a 9x9 inch baking dish, combine the pork and beans, brown sugar, onion, ketchup, mustard, Worcestershire sauce and vinegar and season with salt and pepper to taste. Top with the bacon slices.
3. Bake at 350 degrees F (175 degrees C) for 1 hour, or until sauce is thickened and bacon is cooked.

THAI PEANUT CHICKEN

Servings: 8 | Prep: 25m | Cooks: 15m | Total: 40m

NUTRITION FACTS

Calories: 360 | Carbohydrates: 43.4g | Fat: 11.3g | Protein: 21g | Cholesterol: 34mg

INGREDIENTS

- 2 cups uncooked white rice
- 4 cups water
- 3 tablespoons soy sauce
- 2 tablespoons creamy peanut butter
- 4 skinless, boneless chicken breast halves - cut into thin strips
- 3 tablespoons chopped garlic
- 1 1/2 tablespoons chopped fresh ginger root
- 3/4 cup chopped green onions

- 2 teaspoons white wine vinegar
- 1/4 teaspoon cayenne pepper
- 3 tablespoons olive oil
- 2 1/2 cups broccoli florets
- 1/3 cup unsalted dry-roasted peanuts

DIRECTIONS

1. Combine the rice and water in a saucepan over medium-high heat. Bring to a boil, then reduce heat to low, cover, and simmer for 20 minutes, or until rice is tender. In a small bowl, stir together the soy sauce, peanut butter, vinegar, and cayenne pepper. Set aside.
2. Heat oil in a skillet or wok over high heat. Add chicken, garlic and ginger, and cook, stirring constantly, until chicken is golden on the outside, about 5 minutes.
3. Reduce heat to medium, and add green onion, broccoli, peanuts, and the peanut butter mixture. Cook, stirring frequently, for 5 minutes, or until broccoli is tender, and chicken is cooked through. Serve over rice.

SPICY BAKED SWEET POTATO FRIES

Servings: 6 | Prep: 10m | Cooks: 1h | Total: 1h10m

NUTRITION FACTS

Calories: 169 | Carbohydrates: 29.2g | Fat: 4.7g | Protein: 2.1g | Cholesterol: 0mg

INGREDIENTS

- 6 sweet potatoes, cut into French fries
- 2 tablespoons canola oil
- 3 tablespoons taco seasoning mix
- 1/4 teaspoon cayenne pepper

DIRECTIONS

1. Preheat the oven to 425 degrees F (220 degrees C).
2. In a plastic bag, combine the sweet potatoes, canola oil, taco seasoning, and cayenne pepper. Close and shake the bag until the fries are evenly coated. Spread the fries out in a single layer on two large baking sheets.
3. Bake for 30 minutes, or until crispy and brown on one side. Turn the fries over using a spatula, and cook for another 30 minutes, or until they are all crispy on the outside and tender inside. Thinner fries may not take as long.

BUFFALO CHICKEN FINGERS

Servings: 8 | Prep: 20m | Cooks: 20m | Total: 40m

NUTRITION FACTS

Calories: 125 | Carbohydrates: 10.7g | Fat: 2g | Protein: 15g | Cholesterol: 34mg

INGREDIENTS

- 4 skinless, boneless chicken breast halves - cut into finger-sized pieces
- 1/4 cup all-purpose flour
- 1 teaspoon garlic powder
- 1 teaspoon cayenne pepper
- 1/2 teaspoon salt
- 3/4 cup bread crumbs
- 2 egg whites, beaten
- 1 tablespoon water

DIRECTIONS

1. Preheat oven to 400 degrees F (205 degrees C). Coat a baking sheet with a nonstick spray.
2. In a bag, mix together flour, 1/2 teaspoon garlic powder, 1/2 teaspoon cayenne pepper, and 1/4 teaspoon salt. On a plate, mix the bread crumbs with the rest of the garlic powder, cayenne pepper, and salt.
3. Shake the chicken pieces with the seasoned flour. Beat egg whites with 1 tablespoon water, and place egg mixture in a shallow dish or bowl. Dip seasoned chicken in egg mixture, then roll in the seasoned bread crumb mixture. Place on prepared baking sheet.
4. Bake for about 8 minutes in the preheated oven. Use tongs to turn pieces over. Bake 8 minutes longer, or until chicken juices run clear.

MUSHROOM RICE

Servings: 4 | Prep: 5m | Cooks: 25m | Total: 30m

NUTRITION FACTS

Calories: 216 | Carbohydrates: 41.1g | Fat: 2.8g | Protein: 5.3g | Cholesterol: 8mg

INGREDIENTS

- 2 teaspoons butter
- 6 mushrooms, coarsely chopped
- 2 cups chicken broth
- 1 cup uncooked white rice

- 1 clove garlic, minced
- 1 green onion, finely chopped
- 1/2 teaspoon chopped fresh parsley
- salt and pepper to taste

DIRECTIONS

1. Melt butter in a saucepan over medium heat. Cook mushrooms, garlic and green onion until mushrooms are cooked and liquid has evaporated. Stir in chicken broth and rice. Season with parsley, salt and pepper. Reduce heat, cover and simmer for 20 minutes.

COD WITH ITALIAN CRUMB TOPPING

Servings: 4 | Prep: 15m | Cooks: 10m | Total: 25m

NUTRITION FACTS

Calories: 131 | Carbohydrates: 7g | Fat: 2.9g | Protein: 18.1g | Cholesterol: 39mg

INGREDIENTS

- 1/4 cup fine dry bread crumbs
- 2 tablespoons grated Parmesan cheese
- 1 tablespoon cornmeal
- 1 teaspoon olive oil
- 1/2 teaspoon Italian seasoning
- 1/8 teaspoon garlic powder
- 1/8 teaspoon ground black pepper
- 4 (3 ounce) fillets cod fillets
- 1 egg white, lightly beaten

DIRECTIONS

1. Preheat oven to 450 degrees F (230 degrees C).
2. In a small shallow bowl, stir together the bread crumbs, cheese, cornmeal, oil, italian seasoning, garlic powder and pepper; set aside.
3. Coat the rack of a broiling pan with cooking spray. Place the cod on the rack, folding under any thin edges of the filets. Brush with the egg white, then spoon the crumb mixture evenly on top.
4. Bake in a preheated oven for 10 to 12 minutes or until the fish flakes easily when tested with a fork and is opaque all the way through.

TOMATILLO SALSA VERDE

Servings: 8 | Prep: 10m | Cooks: 15m | Total: 25m

NUTRITION FACTS

Calories: 24 | Carbohydrates: 4.6g | Fat: 0.6g | Protein: 0.8g | Cholesterol: 0mg

INGREDIENTS

- 1 pound tomatillos, husked
- 1/2 cup finely chopped onion
- 1 teaspoon minced garlic
- 1 serrano chile peppers, minced
- 2 tablespoons chopped cilantro
- 1 tablespoon chopped fresh oregano
- 1/2 teaspoon ground cumin
- 1 1/2 teaspoons salt, or to taste
- 2 cups water

DIRECTIONS

1. Place tomatillos, onion, garlic, and chile pepper into a saucepan. Season with cilantro, oregano, cumin, and salt; pour in water. Bring to a boil over high heat, then reduce heat to medium-low, and simmer until the tomatillos are soft, 10 to 15 minutes.
2. Using a blender, carefully puree the tomatillos and water in batches until smooth.

GREEK PASTA WITH TOMATOES AND WHITE BEANS

Servings: 4 | Prep: 10m | Cooks: 15m | Total: 25m

NUTRITION FACTS

Calories: 460 | Carbohydrates: 79g | Fat: 5.9g | Protein: 23.4g | Cholesterol: 17mg

INGREDIENTS

- 2 (14.5 ounce) cans Italian-style diced tomatoes
- 1 (19 ounce) can cannellini beans, drained and rinsed
- 10 ounces fresh spinach, washed and chopped
- 8 ounces penne pasta
- 1/2 cup crumbled feta cheese

DIRECTIONS

1. Cook the pasta in a large pot of boiling salted water until al dente.
2. Meanwhile, combine tomatoes and beans in a large non-stick skillet. Bring to a boil over medium high heat. Reduce heat, and simmer 10 minutes.
3. Add spinach to the sauce; cook for 2 minutes or until spinach wilts, stirring constantly.
4. Serve sauce over pasta, and sprinkle with feta.

AMATRICIANA

Servings: 4 | Prep: 15m | Cooks: 20m | Total: 35m

NUTRITION FACTS

Calories: 529 | Carbohydrates: 97.6g | Fat: 7.5g | Protein: 21.5g | Cholesterol: 12mg

INGREDIENTS

- 4 slices bacon, diced
- 1/2 cup chopped onion
- 1 teaspoon minced garlic
- 1/4 teaspoon crushed red pepper flakes
- 2 (14.5 ounce) cans stewed tomatoes
- 1 pound linguine pasta, uncooked
- 1 tablespoon chopped fresh basil
- 2 tablespoons grated Parmesan cheese

DIRECTIONS

1. Cook diced bacon in a large saucepan over medium high heat until crisp, about 5 minutes. Drain all but 2 tablespoons of drippings from the pan.
2. Add onions, and cook over medium heat about 3 minutes. Stir in garlic and red pepper flakes; cook 30 seconds. Add canned tomatoes, undrained; simmer 10 minutes, breaking up tomatoes.
3. Meanwhile, cook the pasta in a large pot of 4 quarts boiling salted water until al dente. Drain.
4. Stir basil into the sauce, and then toss with cooked pasta. Serve with grated Parmesan cheese.

EASY RED BEANS AND RICE

Servings: 8 | Prep: 10m | Cooks: 30m | Total: 40m

NUTRITION FACTS

Calories: 289 | Carbohydrates: 42.4g | Fat: 5.7g | Protein: 16.3g | Cholesterol: 35mg

INGREDIENTS

- 2 cups water
- 1 cup uncooked rice
- 1 (16 ounce) package turkey kielbasa, cut diagonally into 1/4 inch slices
- 1 onion, chopped
- 1 green bell pepper, chopped
- 1 clove chopped garlic
- 2 (15 ounce) cans canned kidney beans, drained
- 1 (16 ounce) can whole peeled tomatoes, chopped
- 1/2 teaspoon dried oregano
- salt to taste
- 1/2 teaspoon pepper

DIRECTIONS

1. In a saucepan, bring water to a boil. Add rice and stir. Reduce heat, cover and simmer for 20 minutes.
2. In a large skillet over low heat, cook sausage for 5 minutes. Stir in onion, green pepper and garlic; saute until tender. Pour in beans and tomatoes with juice. Season with oregano, salt and pepper. Simmer uncovered for 20 minutes. Serve over rice.

PICO DE GALLO

Servings: 12 | Prep: 20m | Cooks: 3h | Total: 3h20m | Additional: 3h

NUTRITION FACTS

Calories: 10 | Carbohydrates: 2.2g | Fat: 0.1g | Protein: 0.4g | Cholesterol: 0mg

INGREDIENTS

- 6 roma (plum) tomatoes, diced
- 1/2 red onion, minced
- 3 tablespoons chopped fresh cilantro
- 1/2 jalapeno pepper, seeded and minced
- 1/2 lime, juiced
- 1 clove garlic, minced
- 1 pinch garlic powder
- 1 pinch ground cumin, or to taste
- salt and ground black pepper to taste

DIRECTIONS

1. Stir the tomatoes, onion, cilantro, jalapeno pepper, lime juice, garlic, garlic powder, cumin, salt, and pepper together in a bowl. Refrigerate at least 3 hours before serving.

YAKISOBA CHICKEN

Servings: 6 | Prep: 15m | Cooks: 15m | Total: 30m

NUTRITION FACTS

Calories: 295 | Carbohydrates: 40.7g | Fat: 4.8g | Protein: 26.3g | Cholesterol: 46mg

INGREDIENTS

- 1/2 teaspoon sesame oil
- 1 tablespoon canola oil
- 2 tablespoons chile paste
- 2 cloves garlic, chopped
- 4 skinless, boneless chicken breast halves - cut into 1 inch cubes
- 1/2 cup soy sauce
- 1 onion, sliced lengthwise into eighths
- 1/2 medium head cabbage, coarsely chopped
- 2 carrots, coarsely chopped
- 8 ounces soba noodles, cooked and drained

DIRECTIONS

1. In a large skillet combine sesame oil, canola oil and chili paste; stir-fry 30 seconds. Add garlic and stir fry an additional 30 seconds. Add chicken and 1/4 cup of the soy sauce and stir fry until chicken is no longer pink, about 5 minutes. Remove mixture from pan, set aside, and keep warm.
2. In the emptied pan combine the onion, cabbage, and carrots. Stir-fry until cabbage begins to wilt, 2 to 3 minutes. Stir in the remaining soy sauce, cooked noodles, and the chicken mixture to pan and mix to blend. Serve and enjoy!

ANGEL FOOD CAKE

Servings: 14 | Prep: 30m | Cooks: 45m | Total: 1h15m

NUTRITION FACTS

Calories: 136 | Carbohydrates: 29.9g | Fat: 0.1g | Protein: 4g | Cholesterol: 0mg

INGREDIENTS

- 1 cup cake flour
- 1 1/2 cups white sugar
- 12 egg whites
- 1 1/2 teaspoons vanilla extract
- 1 1/2 teaspoons cream of tartar
- 1/2 teaspoon salt

DIRECTIONS

1. Preheat the oven to 375 degrees F (190 degrees C). Be sure that your 10 inch tube pan is clean and dry. Any amount of oil or residue could deflate the egg whites. Sift together the flour, and 3/4 cup of the sugar, set aside.
2. In a large bowl, whip the egg whites along with the vanilla, cream of tartar and salt, to medium stiff peaks. Gradually add the remaining sugar while continuing to whip to stiff peaks. When the egg white mixture has reached its maximum volume, fold in the sifted ingredients gradually, one third at a time. Do not overmix. Put the batter into the tube pan.
3. Bake for 40 to 45 minutes in the preheated oven, until the cake springs back when touched Balance the tube pan upside down on the top of a bottle, to prevent decompression while cooling. When cool, run a knife around the edge of the pan and invert onto a plate.

MANGO SALSA

Servings: 8 | Prep: 15m | Cooks: 30m | Total: 45m | Additional: 30m

NUTRITION FACTS

Calories: 21 | Carbohydrates: 5.4.g | Fat: 0.1g | Protein: 0.3g | Cholesterol: 0mg

INGREDIENTS

- 1 mango - peeled, seeded, and chopped
- 1/4 cup finely chopped red bell pepper
- 1 green onion, chopped
- 2 tablespoons chopped cilantro
- 1 fresh jalapeno chile pepper, finely chopped
- 2 tablespoons lime juice
- 1 tablespoon lemon juice

DIRECTIONS

1. In a medium bowl, mix mango, red bell pepper, green onion, cilantro, jalapeno, lime juice, and lemon juice. Cover, and allow to sit at least 30 minutes before serving.

BLACKENED TILAPIA WITH SECRET HOBO SPICES

Servings: 4 | Prep: 10m | Cooks: 8m | Total: 18m

NUTRITION FACTS

Calories: 245 | Carbohydrates: 21.5g | Fat: 6.8g | Protein: 26.8g | Cholesterol: 42mg

INGREDIENTS

- 3 tablespoons paprika
- 1 tablespoon onion powder
- 1 pinch garlic powder
- 1 teaspoon ground white pepper
- 1 teaspoon ground black pepper
- 1 teaspoon cayenne pepper, or to taste
- 1 teaspoon dried oregano
- 1 teaspoon dried thyme
- 1/2 teaspoon celery seed
- 1 tablespoon kosher salt, or to taste
- 1 pound tilapia fillets
- 1 lemon, cut into wedges
- 4 slices white bread
- 1 tablespoon vegetable oil

DIRECTIONS

1. In a small bowl or jar with a lid, make the spice blend. Mix together the paprika, onion powder, garlic powder, white pepper, black pepper, cayenne pepper, oregano, thyme, celery seed and kosher salt. Coat the fish fillets with the spice mixture, and allow to sit at room temperature for no longer than 30 minutes.
2. Heat a heavy skillet over high heat. Add oil, and heat until it is almost smoking. Place the fillets in the pan, and cook for about 3 minutes per side, or until fish is opaque and can be flaked with a fork. Remove from the pan, and place onto slices of white bread. Pour pan juices over them and squeeze lemon juice all over. Do not underestimate the white bread. It gets quite tasty soaking up all the juices.

PERFECT SUSHI RICE

Servings: 15 | Prep: 5m | Cooks: 20m | Total: 25m

NUTRITION FACTS

Calories: 112 | Carbohydrates: 23.5g | Fat: 1g | Protein: 1.7g | Cholesterol: 0mg

INGREDIENTS

- 2 cups uncooked glutinous white rice (sushi rice)
- 3 cups water
- 1/2 cup rice vinegar
- 1 tablespoon vegetable oil
- 1/4 cup white sugar
- 1 teaspoon salt

DIRECTIONS

1. Rinse the rice in a strainer or colander until the water runs clear. Combine with water in a medium saucepan. Bring to a boil, then reduce the heat to low, cover and cook for 20 minutes. Rice should be tender and water should be absorbed. Cool until cool enough to handle.
2. In a small saucepan, combine the rice vinegar, oil, sugar and salt. Cook over medium heat until the sugar dissolves. Cool, then stir into the cooked rice. When you pour this in to the rice it will seem very wet. Keep stirring and the rice will dry as it cools.

MANGO SALSA

Servings: 8 | Prep: 15m | Cooks: 30m | Total: 45m | Additional: 30m

NUTRITION FACTS

Calories: 21 | Carbohydrates: 5.4g | Fat: 0.1g | Protein: 0.3g | Cholesterol: 0mg

INGREDIENTS

- 1 mango - peeled, seeded, and chopped
- 1/4 cup finely chopped red bell pepper
- 1 green onion, chopped
- 2 tablespoons chopped cilantro
- 1 fresh jalapeno chile pepper, finely chopped
- 2 tablespoons lime juice
- 1 tablespoon lemon juice

DIRECTIONS

1. In a medium bowl, mix mango, red bell pepper, green onion, cilantro, jalapeno, lime juice, and lemon juice. Cover, and allow to sit at least 30 minutes before serving.

MOROCCAN-STYLE STUFFED ACORN SQUASH

Servings: 4 | Prep: 15m | Cooks: 45m | Total: 1h

NUTRITION FACTS

Calories: 502 | Carbohydrates: 93.8g | Fat: 11.7g | Protein: 11.2g | Cholesterol: 10mg

INGREDIENTS

- 2 tablespoons brown sugar
- 1 tablespoon butter, melted
- 2 large acorn squash, halved and seeded
- 2 tablespoons olive oil
- 2 cloves garlic, chopped
- 2 stalks celery, chopped
- 2 carrots, chopped
- 1 cup garbanzo beans, drained
- 1/2 cup raisins
- 1 1/2 tablespoons ground cumin
- salt and pepper to taste
- 1 (14 ounce) can chicken broth
- 1 cup uncooked couscous

DIRECTIONS

1. Preheat oven to 350 degrees F (175 degrees C).
2. Arrange squash halves cut side down on a baking sheet. Bake 30 minutes, or until tender. Dissolve the sugar in the melted butter. Brush squash with the butter mixture, and keep squash warm while preparing the stuffing.
3. Heat the olive oil in a skillet over medium heat. Stir in the garlic, celery, and carrots, and cook 5 minutes. Mix in the garbanzo beans and raisins. Season with cumin, salt, and pepper, and continue to cook and stir until vegetables are tender.
4. Pour the chicken broth into the skillet, and mix in the couscous. Cover skillet, and turn off heat. Allow couscous to absorb liquid for 5 minutes. Stuff squash halves with the skillet mixture to serve.

SLOW COOKER HONEY GARLIC CHICKEN

Servings: 10 | Prep: 20m | Cooks: 4h | Total: 4h20m

NUTRITION FACTS

Calories: 235 | Carbohydrates: 34.4g | Fat: 6g | Protein: 13g | Cholesterol: 42mg

INGREDIENTS

- 1 tablespoon vegetable oil
- 10 boneless, skinless chicken thighs
- 3/4 cup honey
- 3/4 cup lite soy sauce
- 3 tablespoons ketchup
- 2 cloves garlic, crushed
- 1 tablespoon minced fresh ginger root
- 1 (20 ounce) can pineapple tidbits, drained with juice reserved
- 2 tablespoons cornstarch
- 1/4 cup water

DIRECTIONS

1. Heat oil in a skillet over medium heat, and cook chicken thighs just until evenly browned on all sides. Place thighs in a slow cooker.
2. In a bowl, mix honey, soy sauce, ketchup, garlic, ginger, and reserved pineapple juice. Pour into the slow cooker.
3. Cover, and cook 4 hours on High. Stir in pineapple tidbits just before serving.
4. Mix the cornstarch and water in a small bowl. Remove thighs from slow cooker. Blend the cornstarch mixture into remaining sauce in the slow cooker to thicken. Serve sauce over the chicken.

QUICK AND EASY PANCIT

Servings: 6 | Prep: 20m | Cooks: 20m | Total: 40m

NUTRITION FACTS

Calories: 369 | Carbohydrates: 65.1g | Fat: 4.9g | Protein: 18.1g | Cholesterol: 35mg

INGREDIENTS

- 1 (12 ounce) package dried rice noodles
- 1 teaspoon vegetable oil
- 1 small head cabbage, thinly sliced
- 4 carrot, thinly sliced

- 1 onion, finely diced
- 3 cloves garlic, minced
- 2 cups diced cooked chicken breast meat
- 1//4 cup soy sauce
- 2 lemons - cut into wedges, for garnish

DIRECTIONS

1. Place the rice noodles in a large bowl, and cover with warm water. When soft, drain, and set aside.
2. Heat oil in a wok or large skillet over medium heat. Saute onion and garlic until soft. Stir in chicken cabbage, carrots and soy sauce. Cook until cabbage begins to soften. Toss in noodles, and cook until heated through, stirring constantly. Transfer pancit to a serving dish and garnish with quartered lemons.

LENTILS AND SPINACH

Servings: 4 | Prep: 10m | Cooks: 55m | Total: 1h5m

NUTRITION FACTS

Calories: 165 | Carbohydrates: 24g | Fat: 4.3g | Protein: 9.7g | Cholesterol: 0mg

INGREDIENTS

- 1 tablespoon vegetable oil
- 2 white onions, halved and sliced into 1/2 rings
- 3 cloves garlic, minced
- 1/2 cup lentils
- 2 cups water
- 1 (10 ounce) package frozen spinach
- 1 teaspoon salt
- 1 teaspoon ground cumin
- freshly ground black pepper to taste
- 2 cloves garlic, crushed

DIRECTIONS

1. Heat oil in a heavy pan over medium heat. Saute onion for 10 minutes or so, until it begins to turn golden. Add minced garlic and saute for another minute or so.
2. Add lentils and water to the saucepan. Bring mixture to a boil. Cover, lower heat, and simmer about 35 minutes, until lentils are soft (this may take less time, depending on your water and the lentils).

3. Meanwhile cook the spinach in microwave according to package directions. Add spinach, salt and cumin to the saucepan. Cover and simmer until all is heated, about ten minutes. Grind in plenty of pepper and press in extra garlic to taste.

ESPINACAS CON GARBANZOS (SPINACH WITH GARBANZO BEANS)

Servings: 4 | Prep: 15m | Cooks: 10m | Total: 25m

NUTRITION FACTS

Calories: 169 | Carbohydrates: 26g | Fat: 4.9g | Protein: 7.3g | Cholesterol: 0mg

INGREDIENTS

- 1 tablespoon extra-virgin olive oil
- 4 cloves garlic, minced
- 1/2 onion, diced
- 1 (10 ounce) box frozen chopped spinach, thawed and drained well
- 1 (12 ounce) can garbanzo beans, drained
- 1/2 teaspoon cumin
- 1/2 teaspoon salt

DIRECTIONS

1. Heat the olive oil in a skillet over medium-low heat. Cook the garlic and onion in the oil until translucent, about 5 minutes. Stir in the spinach, garbanzo beans, cumin, and salt. Use your stirring spoon to lightly mash the beans as the mixture cooks. Allow to cook until thoroughly heated.

TERRY'S TEXAS PINTO BEANS

Servings: 8 | Prep: 15m | Cooks: 2h | Total: 2h15m

NUTRITION FACTS

Calories: 210 | Carbohydrates: 37.9g | Fat: 1.1g | Protein: 13.2g | Cholesterol: 1mg

INGREDIENTS

- 1 pound dry pinto beans
- 1 (29 ounce) can reduced sodium chicken broth
- 1/2 cup green salsa
- 1 teaspoon cumin

- 1 large onion, chopped
- 1 fresh jalapeno pepper, chopped
- 2 cloves garlic, minced
- 1/2 teaspoon ground black pepper
- water, if needed
-

DIRECTIONS

1. Place the pinto beans in a large pot, and pour in the chicken broth. Stir in onion, jalapeno, garlic, salsa, cumin, and pepper. Bring to a boil, reduce heat to medium-low, and continue cooking 2 hours, stirring often, until beans are tender. Add water as needed to keep the beans moist.

VEGAN BEAN TACO FILLING

Servings: 8 | Prep: 15m | Cooks: 15m | Total: 30m

NUTRITION FACTS

Calories: 142 | Carbohydrates: 24g | Fat: 2.5g | Protein: 7.5g | Cholesterol: 0mg

INGREDIENTS

- 1 tablespoon olive oil
- 1 onion, diced
- 2 cloves garlic, minced
- 1 bell pepper, chopped
- 2 (14.5 ounce) cans black beans, rinsed, drained, and mashed
- 2 tablespoons yellow cornmeal
- 1 1/2 tablespoons cumin
- 1 teaspoon paprika
- 1 teaspoon cayenne pepper
- 1 teaspoon chili powder
- 1 cup salsa

DIRECTIONS

1. Heat olive oil in a medium skillet over medium heat. Stir in onion, garlic, and bell pepper; cook until tender. Stir in mashed beans. Add the cornmeal. Mix in cumin, paprika, cayenne, chili powder, and salsa. Cover, and cook 5 minutes.

BRAZILIAN WHITE RICE

Servings: 8 | Prep: 15m | Cooks: 30m | Total: 45m

NUTRITION FACTS

Calories: 201 | Carbohydrates: 37.5g | Fat: 3.7g | Protein: 3.4g | Cholesterol: 0mg

INGREDIENTS

- 2 cups long-grain white rice
- 2 tablespoons minced onion
- 2 cloves garlic, minced
- 2 tablespoons vegetable oil
- 1 teaspoon salt
- 4 cups hot water

DIRECTIONS

1. Place the rice in a colander and rinse thoroughly with cold water; set aside.
2. Heat the oil in a saucepan over medium heat. Cook the onion in the oil for one minute. Stir in the garlic and cook until the garlic is golden brown. Add the rice and salt and cook and stir until the rice begins to brown. Pour hot water over rice mixture and stir. Reduce heat to low, cover the saucepan, and allow to simmer until the water has been absorbed, 20 to 25 minutes.

GINGERBREAD BISCOTTI

Servings: 48 | Prep: 25m | Cooks: 40m | Total: 1h5m

NUTRITION FACTS

Calories: 70 | Carbohydrates: 12.1g | Fat: 2g | Protein: 1.4g | Cholesterol: 12mg

INGREDIENTS

- 1/3 cup vegetable oil
- 1 cup white sugar
- 3 eggs
- 1/4 cup molasses
- 2 1/4 cups all-purpose flour
- 1 cup whole wheat flour
- 1 tablespoon baking powder
- 1 1/2 tablespoons ground ginger
- 3/4 tablespoon ground cinnamon
- 1/2 tablespoon ground cloves
- 1/4 teaspoon ground nutmeg

DIRECTIONS

1. Preheat the oven to 375 degrees F (190 degrees C). Grease a cookie sheet.
2. In a large bowl, mix together oil, sugar, eggs, and molasses. In another bowl, combine flours, baking powder, ginger, cinnamon, cloves, and nutmeg; mix into egg mixture to form a stiff dough.
3. Divide dough in half, and shape each half into a roll the length of the cookie. Place rolls on cookie sheet, and pat down to flatten the dough to 1/2 inch thickness.
4. Bake in preheated oven for 25 minutes. Remove from oven, and set aside to cool.
5. When cool enough to touch, cut into 1/2 inch thick diagonal slices. Place sliced biscotti on cookie sheet, and bake an additional 5 to 7 minutes on each side, or until toasted and crispy.

SPICED SLOW COOKER APPLESAUCE

Servings: 8 | Prep: 10m | Cooks: 6h30m | Total: 6h40m

NUTRITION FACTS

Calories: 150 | Carbohydrates: 39.4g | Fat: 0.2g | Protein: 0.4g | Cholesterol: 0mg

INGREDIENTS

- 8 apples - peeled, cored, and thinly sliced
- 3/4 cup packed brown sugar
- 1/2 cup water
- 1/2 teaspoon pumpkin pie spice

DIRECTIONS

1. Combine the apples and water in a slow cooker; cook on Low for 6 to 8 hours. Stir in the brown sugar and pumpkin pie spice; continue cooking another 30 minutes.

MEDITERRANEAN KALE

Servings: 6 | Prep: 15m | Cooks: 10m | Total: 25m

NUTRITION FACTS

Calories: 91 | Carbohydrates: 14.5g | Fat: 3.2g | Protein: 4.6g | Cholesterol: 0mg

INGREDIENTS

- 12 cups chopped kale
- 2 tablespoons lemon juice
- 1 tablespoon olive oil, or as needed
- 1 tablespoon minced garlic
- 1 teaspoon soy sauce
- salt to taste
- ground black pepper to taste

DIRECTIONS

1. Place a steamer insert into a saucepan, and fill with water to just below the bottom of the steamer. Cover, and bring the water to a boil over high heat. Add the kale, recover, and steam until just tender, 7 to 10 minutes depending on thickness.
2. Whisk together the lemon juice, olive oil, garlic, soy sauce, salt, and black pepper in a large bowl. Toss steamed kale into dressing until well coated.

PASTA WITH SCALLOPS, ZUCCHINI, AND TOMATOES

Servings: 8 | Prep: 15m | Cooks: 15m | Total: 30m

NUTRITION FACTS

Calories: 335 | Carbohydrates: 46.1g | Fat: 9.1g | Protein: 18.7g | Cholesterol: 20mg

INGREDIENTS

- 1 pound dry fettuccine pasta
- 1/4 cup olive oil
- 3 cloves garlic, minced
- 2 zucchinis, diced
- 1/2 teaspoon salt
- 1/2 teaspoon crushed red pepper flakes
- 1 cup chopped fresh basil
- 4 roma (plum) tomatoes, chopped
- 1 pound bay scallops
- 2 tablespoons grated Parmesan cheese

DIRECTIONS

1. In a large pot with boiling salted water cook pasta until al dente. Drain.

2. Meanwhile, in a large skillet heat oil, add garlic and cook until tender. Add the zucchini, salt, red pepper flakes, dried basil (if using) and saute for 10 minutes. Add chopped tomatoes, bay scallops, and fresh basil (if using) and simmer for 5 minutes, or until scallops are opaque.
3. Pour sauce over cooked pasta and serve with grated Parmesan cheese.

ONE SKILLET MEXICAN QUINOA

Servings: 4 | Prep: 15m | Cooks: 25m | Total: 40m

NUTRITION FACTS

Calories: 450 | Carbohydrates: 67.1g | Fat: 14.9g | Protein: 16.5g | Cholesterol: 2mg

INGREDIENTS

- 1 tablespoon olive oil
- 1 jalapeno pepper, chopped
- 2 cloves garlic, chopped
- 1 (15 ounce) can black beans, rinsed and drained
- 1 (14.5 ounce) can fire-roasted diced tomatoes
- 1 cup yellow corn
- 1 cup quinoa
- 1 cup chicken broth
- 1 tablespoon red pepper flakes, or to taste
- 1 1/2 teaspoons chili powder
- 1/2 teaspoon cumin
- 1 pinch kosher salt and ground black pepper to taste
- 1 avocado - peeled, pitted, and diced
- 1 lime, juiced
- 2 tablespoons chopped fresh cilantro

DIRECTIONS

1. Heat oil in a large skillet over medium-high heat. Saute jalapeno pepper and garlic in hot oil until fragrant, about 1 minute.
2. Stir black beans, tomatoes, yellow corn, quinoa, and chicken broth into skillet; season with red pepper flakes, chili powder, cumin, salt, and black pepper. Bring to a boil, cover the skillet with a lid, reduce heat to low, and simmer until quinoa is tender and liquid is mostly absorbed, about 20 minutes. Stir avocado, lime juice, and cilantro into quinoa until combined.

CAJUN STYLE BAKED SWEET POTATO

Servings: 4 | Prep: 10m | Cooks: 1h | Total: 1h10m

NUTRITION FACTS

Calories: 229 | Carbohydrates: 49.1g | Fat: 2.3g | Protein: 4.8g | Cholesterol: 0mg

INGREDIENTS

- 1 1/2 teaspoons paprika
- 1 teaspoon brown sugar
- 1/4 teaspoon black pepper
- 1/4 teaspoon onion powder
- 1/4 teaspoon dried thyme
- 1/4 teaspoon dried rosemary
- 1/4 teaspoon garlic powder
- 1/8 teaspoon cayenne pepper
- 2 large sweet potatoes
- 1 1/2 teaspoons olive oil

DIRECTIONS

1. Preheat oven to 375 degrees F (190 degrees C).
2. In a small bowl, stir together paprika, brown sugar, black pepper, onion powder, thyme, rosemary, garlic powder, and cayenne pepper.
3. Slice the sweet potatoes in half lengthwise. Brush each half with olive oil. Rub the seasoning mix over the cut surface of each half. Place sweet potatoes on a baking sheet, or in a shallow pan.
4. Bake in preheated oven until tender, or about 1 hour.

SPICY PEACH-GLAZED PORK CHOPS

Servings: 4 | Prep: 10m | Cooks: 20m | Total: 30m

NUTRITION FACTS

Calories: 404 | Carbohydrates: 58.2g | Fat: 11.5g | Protein: 13.2g | Cholesterol: 36mg

INGREDIENTS

- 1 cup peach preserves
- 1 1/2 tablespoons Worcestershire sauce
- 1/2 teaspoon chile paste
- 1 pinch ground cinnamon
- salt and pepper to taste
- 2 tablespoons vegetable oil

- 4 boneless pork chops
- 1/2 cup white wine
- 1 teaspoon ground ginger

DIRECTIONS

1. In a small bowl, mix together the peach preserves, Worcestershire sauce, and chile paste. Rinse pork chops, and pat dry. Sprinkle the chops with ginger, cinnamon, salt, and pepper.
2. Heat oil in a large skillet over medium-high heat. Sear the chops for about 2 minutes on each side. Remove from the pan, and set aside.
3. Pour white wine into the pan, and stir to scrape the bottom of the pan. Stir in the peach preserves mixture. Return the chops to the pan, and flip to coat with the sauce. Reduce heat to medium low, and cook the pork chops for about 8 minutes on each side, or until done.

AUTHENTIC FRENCH MERINGUES

Servings: 36 | Prep: 20m | Cooks: 3h | Total: 3h20m

NUTRITION FACTS

Calories: 31 | Carbohydrates: 7.5g | Fat: 0g | Protein: 0.4g | Cholesterol: 0mg

INGREDIENTS

- 4 egg whites
- 2 1/4 cups confectioners' sugar

DIRECTIONS

1. Preheat the oven to 200 degrees F (95 degrees C). Butter and flour a baking sheet.
2. In a glass or metal bowl, whip egg whites until foamy using an electric mixer. Sprinkle in sugar a little at a time, while continuing to whip at medium speed. When the mixture becomes stiff and shiny like satin, stop mixing, and transfer the mixture to a large pastry bag. Pipe the meringue out onto the prepared baking sheet using a large round tip or star tip.
3. Place the meringues in the oven and place a wooden spoon handle in the door to keep it from closing all the way. Bake for 3 hours, or until the meringues are dry, and can easily be removed from the pan. Allow cookies to cool completely before storing in an airtight container at room temperature.

BAKED FRENCH FRIES

Servings: 4 | Prep: 20m | Cooks: 25m | Total: 45m

NUTRITION FACTS

Calories: 145 | Carbohydrates: 28.2g | Fat: 1.6g | Protein: 5.2g | Cholesterol: 4mg

INGREDIENTS

- 3 russet potatoes, sliced into 1/4 inch strips
- cooking spray
- 1 teaspoon dried basil
- 1/4 cup grated Parmesan cheese
- salt and pepper to taste

DIRECTIONS

1. Preheat oven to 400 degrees F (200 degrees C). Lightly grease a medium baking sheet.
2. Arrange potato strips in a single layer on the prepared baking sheet, skin sides down. Spray lightly with cooking spray, and sprinkle with basil, Parmesan cheese, salt and pepper.
3. Bake 25 minutes in the preheated oven, or until golden brown.

SUPERFAST ASPARAGUS

Servings: 3 | Prep: 5m | Cooks: 10m | Total: 15m

NUTRITION FACTS

Calories: 32 | Carbohydrates: 6.3g | Fat: 0.2g | Protein: 3.4g | Cholesterol: 0mg

INGREDIENTS

- 1 pound asparagus
- 1 teaspoon Cajun seasoning

DIRECTIONS

1. Preheat oven to 425 degrees F (220 degrees C).
2. Snap the asparagus at the tender part of the stalk. Arrange spears in one layer on a baking sheet. Spray lightly with nonstick spray; sprinkle with the Cajun seasoning.
3. Bake in the preheated oven until tender, about 10 minutes.

OVEN ROASTED RED POTATOES AND ASPARAGUS

Servings: 6 | Prep: 15m | Cooks: 45m | Total: 1h

NUTRITION FACTS

Calories: 149 | Carbohydrates: 23.5g | Fat: 4.9g | Protein: 4.2g | Cholesterol: 0mg

INGREDIENTS

- 1 1/2 pounds red potatoes, cut into chunks
- 2 tablespoons extra virgin olive oil
- 8 cloves garlic, thinly sliced
- 4 teaspoons dried rosemary
- 4 teaspoons dried thyme
- 2 teaspoons kosher salt
- 1 bunch fresh asparagus, trimmed and cut into 1 inch pieces
- ground black pepper to taste

DIRECTIONS

1. Preheat oven to 425 degrees F (220 degrees C).
2. In a large baking dish, toss the red potatoes with 1/2 the olive oil, garlic, rosemary, thyme, and 1/2 the kosher salt. Cover with aluminum foil.
3. Bake 20 minutes in the preheated oven. Mix in the asparagus, remaining olive oil, and remaining salt. Cover, and continue cooking 15 minutes, or until the potatoes are tender. Increase oven temperature to 450 degrees F (230 degrees C). Remove foil, and continue cooking 5 to 10 minutes, until potatoes are lightly browned. Season with pepper to serve.

QUINOA WITH CHICKPEAS AND TOMATOES

Servings: 6 | Prep: 20m | Cooks: 20m | Total: 40m

NUTRITION FACTS

Calories: 185 | Carbohydrates: 28.8g | Fat: 5.4g | Protein: 6g | Cholesterol: 0mg

INGREDIENTS

- 1 cup quinoa
- 1/8 teaspoon salt
- 1 3/4 cups water
- 3 tablespoons lime juice
- 4 teaspoons olive oil
- 1/2 teaspoon ground cumin

- 1 cup canned garbanzo beans (chickpeas), drained
- 1 tomato, chopped
- 1 clove garlic, minced
- 1 pinch salt and pepper to taste
- 1/2 teaspoon chopped fresh parsley

DIRECTIONS

1. Place the quinoa in a fine mesh strainer, and rinse under cold, running water until the water no longer foams. Bring the quinoa, salt, and water to a boil in a saucepan. Reduce heat to medium-low, cover, and simmer until the quinoa is tender, 20 to 25 minutes.
2. Once done, stir in the garbanzo beans, tomatoes, garlic, lime juice, and olive oil. Season with cumin, salt, and pepper. Sprinkle with chopped fresh parsley to serve.

JAMIE'S SWEET AND EASY CORN ON THE COB

Servings: 6 | Prep: 5m | Cooks: 10m | Total: 15m

NUTRITION FACTS

Calories: 94 | Carbohydrates: 21.5g | Fat: 1.1g | Protein: 2.9g | Cholesterol: 0mg

INGREDIENTS

- 2 tablespoons white sugar
- 1 tablespoon lemon juice
- 6 ears corn on the cob, husks and silk removed
-

DIRECTIONS

1. Fill a large pot about 3/4 full of water and bring to a boil. Stir in sugar and lemon juice, dissolving the sugar. Gently place ears of corn into boiling water, cover the pot, turn off the heat, and let the corn cook in the hot water until tender, about 10 minutes.

ANGEL HAIR PASTA CHICKEN

Servings: 6 | Prep: 10m | Cooks: 20m | Total: 30m

NUTRITION FACTS

Calories: 282 | Carbohydrates: 34.7g | Fat: 8.4g | Protein: 17.7g | Cholesterol: 28mg

INGREDIENTS

- 2 tablespoons olive oil, divided
- 2 skinless, boneless chicken breast halves - cubed
- 12 ounces angel hair pasta
- 1 carrot, sliced diagonally into 1/4 inch thick slices
- 1 (10 ounce) package frozen broccoli florets, thawed
- 2 cloves garlic, minced
- 2/3 cup chicken broth
- 1 teaspoon dried basil
- 1/4 cup grated Parmesan cheese

DIRECTIONS

1. Heat 1 tablespoon oil in a medium skillet over medium heat. Add chicken and saute for 5 to 7 minutes, or until chicken is cooked through (no longer pink). Remove from skillet and drain on paper towels.
2. Bring a large pot of lightly salted water to a boil. Add pasta and cook for 2 to 4 minutes, or until al dente; drain and set aside.
3. While pasta is cooking, heat 2nd tablespoon oil over medium heat in same skillet used for chicken. Stir fry carrots for about 4 minutes, then add broccoli and garlic and stir fry for another 2 minutes. Finally, stir in broth, basil and cheese and return chicken to skillet. Reduce heat to low and simmer for about 4 minutes.
4. Place drained pasta in a large serving bowl. Top with chicken/vegetable mixture and serve immediately.

INDIAN STYLE BASMATI RICE

Servings: 6 | Prep: 10m | Cooks: 25m | Total: 45m | Additional: 10m

NUTRITION FACTS

Calories: 216 | Carbohydrates: 38.9g | Fat: 5.4g | Protein: 3.9g | Cholesterol: 0mg

INGREDIENTS

- 1 1/2 cups basmati rice
- 2 tablespoons vegetable oil
- 1 (2 inch) piece cinnamon stick
- 2 pods green cardamom
- 1 tablespoon cumin seed
- 1 teaspoon salt, or to taste
- 2 1/2 cups water
- 1 small onion, thinly sliced

- 2 whole cloves

DIRECTIONS

1. Place rice into a bowl with enough water to cover. Set aside to soak for 20 minutes.
2. Heat the oil in a large pot or saucepan over medium heat. Add the cinnamon stick, cardamom pods, cloves, and cumin seed. Cook and stir for about a minute, then add the onion to the pot. Saute the onion until a rich golden brown, about 10 minutes. Drain the water from the rice, and stir into the pot. Cook and stir the rice for a few minutes, until lightly toasted. Add salt and water to the pot, and bring to a boil. Cover, and reduce heat to low. Simmer for about 15 minutes, or until all of the water has been absorbed. Let stand for 5 minutes, then fluff with a fork before serving.

ALFREDO LIGHT

Servings: 8 | Prep: 20m | Cooks: 20m | Total: 40m

NUTRITION FACTS

Calories: 292 | Carbohydrates: 50.5g | Fat: 4.1g | Protein: 13.9g | Cholesterol: 6mg

INGREDIENTS

- 1 onion, chopped
- 1 clove garlic, minced
- 2 teaspoons vegetable oil
- 2 cups skim milk
- 1 cup chicken broth
- 3 tablespoons all-purpose flour
- 1/2 teaspoon salt
- 1/4 teaspoon ground black pepper
- 1/2 cup grated Parmesan cheese
- 16 ounces dry fettuccine pasta
- 1 (16 ounce) package frozen broccoli florets

DIRECTIONS

1. In a medium saucepan, heat oil over medium heat. Add onion and garlic, and saute until golden brown.
2. In a small saucepan, stir together milk, chicken broth, flour, salt and pepper over low heat until smooth and thick. Stir into onion mixture. Continue to cook over medium low heat, stirring frequently, until the sauce is thick. Stir in Parmesan cheese.
3. Meanwhile, cook pasta in boiling water. Add broccoli to the pasta for the last several minutes of cooking. Continue cooking until the pasta is al dente.

4. Drain the pasta and vegetables, and transfer to a large bowl. Toss with sauce. Serve.

OVEN FRIES

Servings: 6 | Prep: 15m | Cooks: 30m | Total: 45m

NUTRITION FACTS

Calories: 156 | Carbohydrates: 34.1g | Fat: 1g | Protein: 3.8g | Cholesterol: 0mg

INGREDIENTS

- 2 1/2 pounds baking potatoes
- 1 teaspoon vegetable oil
- 1 tablespoon white sugar
- 1 teaspoon salt
- 1 pinch ground cayenne pepper

DIRECTIONS

1. Preheat oven to 450 degrees F (230 degrees C). Line a baking sheet with foil, and coat well with vegetable cooking spray. Scrub potatoes well and cut into 1/2 inch thick fries.
2. In a large mixing bowl, toss potatoes with oil, sugar, salt and red pepper. Spread on baking sheet in one layer.
3. Bake for 30 minutes in the preheated oven, until potatoes are tender and browned. Serve immediately.

SWEET AND SOUR SAUCE

Servings: 48 | Prep: 5m | Cooks: 15m | Total: 20m

NUTRITION FACTS

Calories: 32 | Carbohydrates: 8.1g | Fat: 0g | Protein: 0.2g | Cholesterol: 0mg

INGREDIENTS

- 2 cups water
- 2/3 cup distilled white vinegar
- 1 1/2 cups white sugar
- 1 (6 ounce) can tomato paste
- 1 (8 ounce) can pineapple tidbits, drained
- 3 tablespoons cornstarch

DIRECTIONS

1. In a medium saucepan over medium heat, mix together water, distilled white vinegar, white sugar, tomato paste, pineapple tidbits and cornstarch. Cook, stirring occasionally, 15 minutes, or until mixture reaches desired color and consistency.

BUTTERNUT SQUASH FRIES

Servings: 4 | Prep: 15m | Cooks: 20m | Total: 35m

NUTRITION FACTS

Calories: 102 | Carbohydrates: 26.5g | Fat: 0.2g | Protein: 2.3g | Cholesterol: 0mg

INGREDIENTS

- 1 (2 pound) butternut squash, halved and seeded
- salt to taste

DIRECTIONS

1. Preheat the oven to 425 degrees F (220 degrees C).
2. Use a sharp knife to carefully cut away the peel from the squash. Cut the squash into sticks like French fries. Arrange squash pieces on a baking sheet and season with salt.
3. Bake for 20 minutes in the preheated oven, turning the fries over halfway through baking. Fries are done when they are starting to brown on the edges and become crispy.

UNSLOPPY JOES

Servings: 8 | Prep: 15m | Cooks: 15m | Total: 30m

NUTRITION FACTS

Calories: 204 | Carbohydrates: 34.6g | Fat: 3.9g | Protein: 7.8g | Cholesterol: 0mg

INGREDIENTS

- 1 tablespoon olive oil
- 1/2 cup chopped onion
- 1/2 cup chopped celery
- 1/2 cup chopped carrots
- 1 1/2 tablespoons chili powder
- 1 tablespoon tomato paste
- 1 tablespoon distilled white vinegar
- 1 teaspoon ground black pepper

- 1/2 cup chopped green bell pepper
- 1 clove garlic, minced
- 1 (14.5 ounce) can diced tomatoes
- 1 (15 ounce) can kidney beans, drained and rinsed
- 8 kaiser rolls

DIRECTIONS

1. Heat olive oil in a large skillet over medium heat. Add onion, celery, carrot, green pepper, and garlic: saute until tender. Stir in tomatoes, chili powder, tomato paste, vinegar, and pepper. Cover, reduce heat, and simmer 10 minutes.
2. Stir in kidney beans, and cook an additional 5 minutes.
3. Cut a 1/4 inch slice off the top of each kaiser roll; set aside. Hollow out the center of each roll, leaving about 1/2 inch thick shells; reserve the inside of rolls for other uses.
4. Spoon bean mixture evenly into rolls and replace tops. Serve immediately.

TERIYAKI AND PINEAPPLE CHICKEN

Servings: 8 | Prep: 15m | Cooks: 25m | Total: 40m

NUTRITION FACTS

Calories: 187 | Carbohydrates: 18.1g | Fat: 5.5g | Protein: 16.3g | Cholesterol: 35mg

INGREDIENTS

- 2 tablespoons vegetable oil
- 1 pound skinless, boneless chicken breasts, cut into cubes
- 1 green bell pepper, sliced thin
- 1 yellow bell pepper, sliced thin
- 1 red bell pepper, sliced thin
- 1 1/4 cups sliced fresh mushrooms
- 1 onion, chopped
- 1 cup teriyaki sauce
- 1 (8 ounce) can pineapple chunks, undrained
- 1 teaspoon garlic powder
- 1 teaspoon crushed red pepper
- 1/4 cup all-purpose flour

DIRECTIONS

1. Heat the oil in a wok or large skillet over medium-high heat. Cook the chicken until no longer pink in the center and the juices run clear, 7 to 10 minutes.

2. Place the green bell pepper, yellow bell pepper, red bell pepper, mushrooms, onion, teriyaki sauce, pineapple chunks with the juice, garlic powder, and crushed red pepper into the wok, and turn the heat to medium. Bring to a simmer, stir in the flour, and continue simmering 15 minutes until thickened.

MEXICAN PASTA

Servings: 4 | Prep: 5m | Cooks: 15m | Total: 20m

NUTRITION FACTS

Calories: 358 | Carbohydrates: 59.5g | Fat: 9.4g | Protein: 10.3g | Cholesterol: 0mg

INGREDIENTS

- 1/2 pound seashell pasta
- 2 tablespoons olive oil
- 2 onions, chopped
- 1 green bell pepper, chopped
- 1/2 cup sweet corn kernels
- 1 (15 ounce) can black beans, drained
- 1 (14.5 ounce) can peeled and diced tomatoes
- 1/4 cup salsa
- 1/4 cup sliced black olives
- 1 1/2 tablespoons taco seasoning mix
- salt and pepper to taste

DIRECTIONS

1. Bring a large pot of lightly salted water to a boil. Add pasta and cook for 8 to 10 minutes or until al dente; drain.
2. While pasta is cooking, heat olive oil over medium heat in a large skillet. Cook onions and pepper in oil until lightly browned, 10 minutes. Stir in corn and heat through. Stir in black beans, tomatoes, salsa, olives, taco seasoning and salt and pepper and cook until thoroughly heated, 5 minutes.
3. Toss sauce with cooked pasta and serve.

FRESH SALSA

Servings: 48 | Prep: 20m | Cooks: 15m | Total: 35m

NUTRITION FACTS

Calories: 6 | Carbohydrates: 1.5g | Fat: 0g | Protein: 0.2g | Cholesterol: 0mg

INGREDIENTS

- 4 jalapeno chile peppers
- 5 cloves garlic, finely chopped
- 1 onion, finely chopped
- 1 tablespoon white sugar
- 1 teaspoon salt
- 1/4 teaspoon ground cumin
- 1 (10 ounce) can diced tomatoes with green chile peppers
- 1 (28 ounce) can whole peeled tomatoes

DIRECTIONS

1. Preheat oven to 400 degrees F (200 degrees C).
2. Place jalapeno chile peppers on a medium baking sheet. Bake in the preheated oven 15 minutes, or until roasted. Remove from heat and chop off stems.
3. Place jalapeno chile peppers, garlic, onion, white sugar, salt, ground cumin and diced tomatoes with green chile peppers in a blender or food processor. Chop using the pulse setting for a few seconds. Mix in whole peeled tomatoes. Chop using the pulse setting to attain desired consistency. Transfer to a medium bowl. Cover and chill in the refrigerator until serving.

ROASTED VEGETABLE MEDLEY

Servings: 6 | Prep: 25m | Cooks: 1h | Total: 1h55m | Additional: 30m

NUTRITION FACTS

Calories: 191 | Carbohydrates: 34.6g | Fat: 5g | Protein: 4g | Cholesterol: 0mg

INGREDIENTS

- 2 tablespoons olive oil, divided
- 1 large yam, peeled and cut into 1 inch pieces
- 1 large parsnip, peeled and cut into 1 inch pieces
- 1 cup baby carrots
- 1 zucchini, cut into 1 inch slices
- 1 bunch fresh asparagus, trimmed and cut into 1 inch pieces
- 1/2 cup roasted red peppers, cut into 1-inch pieces
- 2 cloves garlic, minced
- 1/4 cup chopped fresh basil
- 1/2 teaspoon kosher salt
- 1/2 teaspoon ground black pepper

DIRECTIONS

1. Preheat oven to 425 degrees F (220 degrees C). Grease 2 baking sheets with 1 tablespoon olive oil.
2. Place the yams, parsnips, and carrots onto the baking sheets. Bake in the preheated oven for 30 minutes, then add the zucchini and asparagus, and drizzle with the remaining 1 tablespoon of olive oil. Continue baking until all of the vegetables are tender, about 30 minutes more. Once tender, remove from the oven, and allow to cool for 30 minutes on the baking sheet.
3. Toss the roasted peppers together with the garlic, basil, salt, and pepper in a large bowl until combined. Add the roasted vegetables, and toss to mix. Serve at room temperature or cold.

ASPARAGUS, CHICKEN AND PENNE PASTA

Servings: 8 | Prep: 15m | Cooks: 20m | Total: 35m

NUTRITION FACTS

Calories: 311 | Carbohydrates: 43.2g | Fat: 6.8g | Protein: 20.3g | Cholesterol: 29mg

INGREDIENTS

- 1 (16 ounce) package dry penne pasta
- 2 tablespoons olive oil, divided
- 3/4 pound skinless, boneless chicken breast meat - cut into bite-size pieces
- 4 cloves garlic, minced
- 12 ounces asparagus, trimmed and cut into 1 inch pieces
- 1 teaspoon crushed red pepper flakes
- salt and pepper to taste
- 1/2 cup grated Parmesan cheese

DIRECTIONS

1. Bring a large pot of lightly salted water to a boil. Cook pasta in boiling water for 8 to 10 minutes, or until al dente. Drain, and transfer to a large bowl.
2. Heat 1 tablespoon olive oil in a large skillet over medium heat. Saute chicken until firm and lightly browned; remove from pan. Add the remaining tablespoon of olive oil to the skillet. Cook and stir garlic, asparagus, and red pepper flakes in oil until asparagus is tender. Stir in chicken, and cook for 2 minutes to blend the flavors. Season with salt and pepper.
3. Toss pasta with chicken and asparagus mixture. Sprinkle with Parmesan cheese.

FABULOUS FAJITAS

Servings: 10 | Prep: 15m | Cooks: 15m | Total: 30m

NUTRITION FACTS

Calories: 427 | Carbohydrates: 64.2g | Fat: 10.3g | Protein: 18g | Cholesterol: 21mg

INGREDIENTS

- 2 green bell peppers, sliced
- 1 red bell pepper, sliced
- 1 onion, thinly sliced
- 1 cup fresh sliced mushrooms
- 2 cups diced, cooked chicken meat
- 1 (.7 ounce) package dry Italian-style salad dressing mix
- 10 (12 inch) flour tortillas

DIRECTIONS

1. Cut peppers and onion into thin slices. Do not dice, leave slices long and thin.
2. Saute peppers and onion in a small amount of oil until tender. Add mushrooms and chicken. Continue to cook on low heat until heated through. Stir in dry salad dressing mix and blend thoroughly.
3. Warm tortillas and roll mixture inside. If desired top with shredded cheddar cheese, diced tomato and shredded lettuce.

MARIA'S MEXICAN RICE

Servings: 6 | Prep: 10m | Cooks: 30m | Total: 40m

NUTRITION FACTS

Calories: 164 | Carbohydrates: 26.8g | Fat: 4.9g | Protein: 2.7g | Cholesterol: 0mg

INGREDIENTS

- 2 tablespoons olive oil
- 1 cup rice
- 1/2 large onion, diced
- 1/2 tablespoon salt
- 1/8 teaspoon ground black pepper
- 2 1/2 cups water
- 1/3 cup tomato sauce
- 1 tablespoon chicken bouillon (such as Knorr®)

- 1/8 teaspoon ground cumin
- 1 whole serrano chile pepper (optional)

DIRECTIONS

1. Heat oil in a saucepan over medium heat. Cook and stir rice and onion in the hot oil until browned, about 5 minutes; season with salt, cumin, and pepper. Pour water over the rice mixture. Stir tomato sauce and chicken bouillon into the water. Increase heat to medium-high, place a cover on the saucepan, and bring to a boil. Add serrano chile pepper and continue cooking at a boil for 10 minutes. Reduce heat to medium-low until the rice is tender and the water is absorbed, 15 to 20 minutes more.

PEPPERED BACON AND TOMATO LINGUINE

Servings: 6 | Prep: 15m | Cooks: 15m | Total: 30m

NUTRITION FACTS

Calories: 362 | Carbohydrates: 57.5g | Fat: 7.6g | Protein: 16.2g | Cholesterol: 16mg

INGREDIENTS

- 1/2 pound peppered bacon, diced
- 2 tablespoons chopped green onion
- 2 teaspoons minced garlic
- 1 (14.5 ounce) can diced tomatoes
- 1 teaspoon dried basil
- 1 teaspoon salt
- ground black pepper to taste
- 1 (16 ounce) package linguine pasta
- 3 tablespoons grated Parmesan cheese

DIRECTIONS

1. Place bacon in a large, deep skillet. Cook over medium high heat until evenly brown. Drain, reserving drippings, and set aside.
2. Saute green onion and garlic in bacon drippings over medium heat for one minute. Stir in tomatoes, basil, salt and ground black pepper; simmer for 5 minutes.
3. Meanwhile, bring a large pot of lightly salted water to a boil. Add pasta and cook for 8 to 10 minutes or until al dente; drain.
4. Toss hot pasta with sauce and sprinkle with Parmesan cheese.

BAKED POTATO

Servings: 1 | Prep: 3m | Cooks: 1h30m | Total: 1h33m

NUTRITION FACTS

Calories: 128 | Carbohydrates: 29.7g | Fat: 0.1g | Protein: 2.7g | Cholesterol: 0mg

INGREDIENTS

- 1 baking potato

DIRECTIONS

1. Preheat oven to 350 degrees F (175 degrees C).
2. Scrub the potato and prick it with a fork to prevent steam from building up and causing the potato to explode in your oven.
3. Bake for 1 1/2 hours.

SLOW COOKER HOMEMADE BEANS

Servings: 12 | Prep: 20m | Cooks: 10h | Total: 10h20m

NUTRITION FACTS

Calories: 296 | Carbohydrates: 57g | Fat: 3g | Protein: 12.4g | Cholesterol: 5mg

INGREDIENTS

- 3 cups dry navy beans, soaked overnight or boiled for one hour
- 1 1/2 cups ketchup
- 1 1/2 cups water
- 1/4 cup molasses
- 1 large onion, chopped
- 1 tablespoon dry mustard
- 1 tablespoon salt
- 6 slices thick cut bacon, cut into 1 inch pieces
- 1 cup brown sugar

DIRECTIONS

1. Drain soaking liquid from beans, and place them in a Slow Cooker.

2. Stir ketchup, water, molasses, onion, mustard, salt, bacon, and brown sugar into the beans until well mixed.
3. Cover, and cook on LOW for 8 to 10 hours, stirring occasionally if possible, though not necessary.

BUTTERNUT SQUASH PIZZAS WITH ROSEMARY

Servings: 4 | Prep: 20m | Cooks: 30m | Total: 50m

NUTRITION FACTS

Calories: 567 | Carbohydrates: 96.9g | Fat: 13.7g | Protein: 14.8g | Cholesterol: 3mg

INGREDIENTS

- 1 cup thinly sliced onion
- 1/2 butternut squash - peeled, seeded, and thinly sliced
- 1 teaspoon chopped fresh rosemary
- salt and black pepper to taste
- 3 tablespoons olive oil, divided
- 1 (16 ounce) package refrigerated pizza crust dough, divided
- 1 tablespoon cornmeal
- 2 tablespoons grated Asiago or Parmesan cheese

DIRECTIONS

1. Preheat oven to 400 degrees F (205 degrees C). Place sliced onion and squash in a roasting pan. Sprinkle with rosemary, salt, pepper, and 2 tablespoons of the olive oil; toss to coat.
2. Bake in the preheated oven for 20 minutes, or until onions are lightly browned and squash is tender; set aside.
3. Increase oven temperature to 450 degrees F (230 degrees C). On a floured surface, roll each ball of dough into an 8 inch round. Place the rounds on a baking sheet sprinkled with cornmeal (you may need 2 baking sheets depending on their size). Distribute squash mixture over the two rounds and continue baking for 10 minutes, checking occasionally, or until the crust is firm. Sprinkle with cheese and remaining tablespoon olive oil. Cut into quarters, and serve.

QUICK BLACK BEANS AND RICE

Servings: 4 | Prep: 5m | Cooks: 15m | Total: 25m

NUTRITION FACTS

Calories: 271 | Carbohydrates: 47.8g | Fat: 5.3g | Protein: 10g | Cholesterol: 0mg

INGREDIENTS

- 1 tablespoon vegetable oil
- 1 onion, chopped
- 1 (15 ounce) can black beans, undrained
- 1 (14.5 ounce) can stewed tomatoes
- 1 teaspoon dried oregano
- 1/2 teaspoon garlic powder
- 1 1/2 cups uncooked instant brown rice

DIRECTIONS

1. In large saucepan, heat oil over medium-high. Add onion, cook and stir until tender. Add beans, tomatoes, oregano and garlic powder. Bring to a boil; stir in rice. Cover; reduce heat and simmer 5 minutes. Remove from heat; let stand 5 minutes before serving.

QUICK TUNA CASSEROLE

Servings: 4 | Prep: 5m | Cooks: 20m | Total: 25m

NUTRITION FACTS

Calories: 363 | Carbohydrates: 46.1g | Fat: 7.1g | Protein: 28.1g | Cholesterol: 26mg

INGREDIENTS

- 1 (7.25 ounce) package macaroni and cheese mix
- 1 (10.75 ounce) can condensed cream of mushroom soup
- 1 (9 ounce) can tuna, drained
- 1 (10 ounce) can peas, drained

DIRECTIONS

1. Prepare macaroni and cheese mix according to package directions. Stir in the cream of mushroom soup, tuna and peas. Mix well, and heat until bubbly.

SPINACH CHICKPEA CURRY

Servings: 4 | Prep: 5m | Cooks: 15m | Total: 20m

NUTRITION FACTS

Calories: 346 | Carbohydrates: 44.7g | Fat: 12.3g | Protein: 21.7g | Cholesterol: 0mg

INGREDIENTS

- 1 tablespoon vegetable oil
- 1 onion, chopped
- 1 (14.75 ounce) can creamed corn
- 1 tablespoon curry paste
- salt to taste
- ground black pepper to taste
- 1/2 teaspoon garlic powder, or to taste
- 1 (15 ounce) can garbanzo beans (chickpeas), drained and rinsed
- 1 (12 ounce) package firm tofu, cubed
- 1 bunch fresh spinach, stems removed
- 1 teaspoon dried basil or to taste

DIRECTIONS

1. In a large wok or skillet heat oil over medium heat; saute onions until translucent. Stir in creamed corn and curry paste. Cook, stirring regularly, for 5 minutes. As you stir, add salt, pepper and garlic.
2. Stir in garbanzo beans and gently fold in tofu. Add spinach and cover. When spinach is tender, remove from heat and stir in basil.

SCALLOP SCAMPI

Servings: 8 | Prep: 15m | Cooks: 30m | Total: 45m

NUTRITION FACTS

Calories: 360 | Carbohydrates: 43.5g | Fat: 9.3g | Protein: 21.3g | Cholesterol: 31mg

INGREDIENTS

- 4 tablespoons margarine
- 3 cloves garlic, minced
- 1 large onion, minced
- 1/2 cup dry white wine
- 1 teaspoon salt
- 1/4 teaspoon ground black pepper
- 1/2 cup grated Romano cheese
- 1 (10.75 ounce) can chicken broth
- 1 pound bay scallops
- 1 pound linguine pasta
- 1/4 cup chopped fresh parsley

DIRECTIONS

1. In a large skillet, melt margarine over medium heat and saute garlic and onion until translucent. Add wine, salt, ground black pepper and 1/4 cup cheese.
2. Add chicken broth and scallops; increase heat and boil rapidly for 7 to 8 minutes.
3. Meanwhile, bring a large pot of lightly salted water to a boil. Add pasta and cook for 8 to 10 minutes or until al dente; drain.
4. Reduce heat for scallop mixture and add parsley; place sauce on top of linguine. Sprinkle with remaining cheese; serve.

APPLESAUCE

Servings: 4 | Prep: 20m | Cooks: 15m | Total: 35m

NUTRITION FACTS

Calories: 195 | Carbohydrates: 51g | Fat: 0.3g | Protein: 0.5g | Cholesterol: 0mg

INGREDIENTS

- 6 cups apples - peeled, cored and chopped
- 3/4 cup water
- 1/8 teaspoon ground cinnamon
- 1/8 teaspoon ground cloves
- 1/2 cup white sugar

DIRECTIONS

1. In a 2 quart saucepan over medium heat, combine apples, water, cinnamon, and cloves. Bring to a boil, reduce heat, and simmer 10 minutes. Stir in sugar, and simmer 5 more minutes.

TASTY LENTIL TACOS

Servings: 6 | Prep: 10m | Cooks: 40m | Total: 50m

NUTRITION FACTS

Calories: 304 | Carbohydrates: 44.2g | Fat: 10g | Protein: 9.4g | Cholesterol: 1mg

INGREDIENTS

- 1 teaspoon canola oil
- 2/3 cup finely chopped onion
- 1 tablespoon taco seasoning, or to taste
- 1 2/3 cups chicken broth

- 1 small clove garlic, minced
- 2/3 cup dried lentils, rinsed
- 2/3 cup salsa
- 12 taco shells

DIRECTIONS

1. Heat oil in a skillet over medium heat; cook and stir onion and garlic until tender, about 5 minutes. Mix lentils and taco seasoning into onion mixture; cook and stir for 1 minute.
2. Pour chicken broth into skillet and bring to a boil. Reduce heat to low, cover the skillet, and simmer until lentils are tender, 25 to 30 minutes.
3. Uncover the skillet and cook until mixture is slightly thickened, 6 to 8 minutes. Mash lentils slightly; stir in salsa.
4. Serve about 1/4 cup lentil mixture in each taco shell.

VEGGIE BURGERS

Servings: 8 | Prep: 15m | Cooks: 20m | Total: 1h35m

NUTRITION FACTS

Calories: 193 | Carbohydrates: 31.9g | Fat: 4.3g | Protein: 6.9g | Cholesterol: 27mg

INGREDIENTS

- 2 teaspoons olive oil
- 1 small onion, grated
- 2 cloves crushed garlic
- 2 carrots, shredded
- 1 small summer squash, shredded
- 1 small zucchini, shredded
- 1 1/2 cups rolled oats
- 1/4 cup shredded Cheddar cheese
- 1 egg, beaten
- 1 tablespoon soy sauce
- 1 1/2 cups all-purpose flour

DIRECTIONS

1. Heat the olive oil in a skillet over low heat, and cook the onion and garlic for about 5 minutes, until tender. Mix in the carrots, squash, and zucchini. Continue to cook and stir for 2 minutes. Remove pan from heat, and mix in oats, cheese, and egg. Stir in soy sauce, transfer the mixture to a bowl, and refrigerate 1 hour.
2. Preheat the grill for high heat.
3. Place the flour on a large plate. Form the vegetable mixture into eight 3 inch round patties. Drop each patty into the flour, lightly coating both sides.

4. Oil the grill grate, and grill patties 5 minutes on each side, or until heated through and nicely browned.

TASTY LENTIL TACOS

Servings: 6 | Prep: 10m | Cooks: 40m | Total: 50m

NUTRITION FACTS

Calories: 304 | Carbohydrates: 44.2g | Fat: 10g | Protein: 9.4g | Cholesterol: 1mg

INGREDIENTS

- 1 teaspoon canola oil
- 2/3 cup finely chopped onion
- 1 small clove garlic, minced
- 2/3 cup dried lentils, rinsed
- 1 tablespoon taco seasoning, or to taste
- 1 2/3 cups chicken broth
- 2/3 cup salsa
- 12 taco shells

DIRECTIONS

1. Heat oil in a skillet over medium heat; cook and stir onion and garlic until tender, about 5 minutes. Mix lentils and taco seasoning into onion mixture; cook and stir for 1 minute.
2. Pour chicken broth into skillet and bring to a boil. Reduce heat to low, cover the skillet, and simmer until lentils are tender, 25 to 30 minutes.
3. Uncover the skillet and cook until mixture is slightly thickened, 6 to 8 minutes. Mash lentils slightly; stir in salsa.
4. Serve about 1/4 cup lentil mixture in each taco shell.

MEXICAN RICE

Servings: 8 | Prep: 20m | Cooks: 30m | Total: 50m

NUTRITION FACTS

Calories: 199 | Carbohydrates: 33.8g | Fat: 5.6g | Protein: 3.4g | Cholesterol: 0mg

INGREDIENTS

- 3 tablespoons vegetable oil
- 2/3 cup diced onion
- 1 1/2 cups uncooked white rice
- 1 1/2 (8 ounce) cans tomato sauce
- 2 teaspoons salt
- 1 clove garlic, minced

- 1 cup chopped green bell pepper
- 1 teaspoon ground cumin
- 1 teaspoon chili powder
- 1/8 teaspoon powdered saffron
- 3 cups water
-

DIRECTIONS

1. In a large saucepan, heat vegetable oil over a medium-low heat. Place the onions in the pan, and saute until golden.
2. Add rice to pan, and stir to coat grains with oil. Mix in green bell pepper, cumin, chili powder, tomato sauce, salt, garlic, saffron, and water. Cover, bring to a boil, and then reduce heat to simmer. Cook for 30 to 40 minutes, or until rice is tender. Stir occasionally.

SLOW COOKER BAKED POTATOES

Servings: 4 | Prep: 10m | Cooks: 4h30m | Total: 4h40m

NUTRITION FACTS

Calories: 254 | Carbohydrates: 51.2g | Fat: 3.6g | Protein: 6.1g | Cholesterol: 0mg

INGREDIENTS

- 4 baking potatoes, well scrubbed
- 1 tablespoon extra virgin olive oil
- kosher salt to taste
- 4 sheets aluminum foil

DIRECTIONS

1. Prick the potatoes with a fork several times, then rub potatoes with olive oil, sprinkle with salt, and wrap tightly in foil. Place the potatoes into a slow cooker, cover, and cook on High for 4 1/2 to 5 hours, or on Low for 7 1/2 to 8 hours until tender.

TWELVE MINUTE PASTA TOSS

Servings: 8 | Prep: 20m | Cooks: 12m | Total: 32m

NUTRITION FACTS

Calories: 360 | Carbohydrates: 46.3g | Fat: 10.2g | Protein: 21.4g | Cholesterol: 33mg

INGREDIENTS

- 16 ounces rotini pasta
- 4 tablespoons olive oil
- 4 skinless, boneless chicken breast halves, cut into bite size pieces
- 3 cloves garlic, minced
- 1 1/4 teaspoons salt
- 1 1/4 teaspoons garlic powder
- 1 1/4 teaspoons dried basil
- 1 1/4 teaspoons dried oregano
- 1 cup chopped sun-dried tomatoes
- 1/4 cup grated Parmesan cheese

DIRECTIONS

1. Bring a large pot of lightly salted water to a boil; cook rotini at a boil until tender yet firm to the bite, about 8 minutes; drain.
2. Heat oil in a large pot over medium-high heat. Saute chicken, garlic, salt, garlic powder, basil, and oregano in hot oil until chicken is no longer pink in the middle, 5 to 10 minutes. Add sun-dried tomatoes and cook until heated through, about 2 minutes. Remove from heat.
3. Pour pasta into pot and toss with chicken until combined. Top with Parmesan cheese.

GRILLED CHICKEN BURGERS

Servings: 8 | Prep: 30m | Cooks: 15m | Total: 45m

NUTRITION FACTS

Calories: 486 | Carbohydrates: 104g | Fat: 4.7g | Protein: 14.5g | Cholesterol: 23mg

INGREDIENTS

- 1 onion, chopped
- 2 teaspoons minced garlic
- 1 red bell pepper, chopped
- 1 cup fresh sliced mushrooms
- 1 tomato, seeded and chopped
- 2 carrots, chopped
- 2 pounds ground chicken
- 1 egg
- 1/2 cup fresh bread crumbs
- 1 tablespoon Old Bay ™ Seasoning
- kosher salt to taste
- black pepper to taste

DIRECTIONS

1. Preheat an outdoor grill for medium heat and lightly oil grate.
2. Lightly spray a saute pan with cooking or oil spray over medium heat. Saute the onion with the garlic first, then the bell pepper, then the mushrooms, tomatoes and carrots, all to desired tenderness. Set aside and allow all vegetables to cool completely.
3. In a large bowl, combine the chicken and vegetables. Add the egg, bread crumbs and seasonings to taste. Mix all together well and form into 8 patties.
4. Grill over medium heat for 5 to 6 minutes per side, or to desired doneness.

GRILLED CILANTRO SALMON

Servings: 6 | Prep: 15m | Cooks: 20m | Total: 45m

NUTRITION FACTS

Calories: 459 | Carbohydrates: 94.3g | Fat: 4.5g | Protein: 17g | Cholesterol: 34mg

INGREDIENTS

- 1 bunch cilantro leaves, chopped
- 2 cloves garlic, chopped
- 2 cups honey
- juice from one lime
- 4 salmon steaks
- salt and pepper to taste

DIRECTIONS

1. In a small saucepan over medium-low heat, stir together cilantro, garlic, honey, and lime juice. Heat until the honey is easily stirred, about 5 minutes. Remove from heat, and let cool slightly.
2. Place salmon steaks in a baking dish, and season with salt and pepper. Pour marinade over salmon, cover, and refrigerate 10 minutes.
3. Preheat an outdoor grill for high heat.
4. Lightly oil grill grate. Place salmon steaks on grill, cook 5 minutes on each side, or until fish is easily flaked with a fork.

JAPANESE BEEF STIR-FRY

Servings: 8 | Prep: 30m | Cooks: 15m | Total: 45m

NUTRITION FACTS

Calories: 290 | Carbohydrates: 26.4g | Fat: 7.6g | Protein: 26.4g | Cholesterol: 39mg

INGREDIENTS

- 2 pounds boneless beef sirloin or beef top round steaks (3/4" thick)
- 3 tablespoons cornstarch
- 1 (10.5 ounce) can Campbell's® Condensed Beef Broth
- 1/2 cup soy sauce
- 2 tablespoons sugar
- 2 tablespoons vegetable oil
- 4 cups sliced shiitake mushrooms
- 1 head Chinese cabbage (bok choy), thinly sliced
- 2 medium red peppers, cut into 2"-long strips
- 3 stalks celery, sliced
- 2 medium green onions, cut into 2" pieces
- Hot cooked regular long-grain white rice

DIRECTIONS

1. Slice beef into very thin strips.
2. Mix cornstarch, broth, soy and sugar until smooth. Set aside.
3. Heat 1 tablespoon oil in saucepot or wok over high heat. Add beef in 2 batches and stir-fry until browned. Set beef aside.
4. Add 1 tablespoon oil. Add the mushrooms, cabbage, peppers, celery and green onions in 2 batches and stir-fry over medium heat until tender-crisp. Set vegetables aside.
5. Stir cornstarch mixture and add. Cook until mixture boils and thickens, stirring constantly. Return beef and vegetables to saucepot and heat through. Serve over rice.

ROASTED GREEN BEANS

Servings: 4 | Prep: 10m | Cooks: 20m | Total: 30m

NUTRITION FACTS

Calories: 101 | Carbohydrates: 16.4g | Fat: 3.7g | Protein: 4.2g | Cholesterol: 0mg

INGREDIENTS

- 2 pounds fresh green beans, trimmed
- 1 tablespoon olive oil, or as needed
- 1 teaspoon kosher salt
- 1/2 teaspoon freshly ground black pepper

DIRECTIONS

1. Preheat oven to 400 degrees F (200 degrees C).
2. Pat green beans dry with paper towels if necessary; spread onto a jellyroll pan. Drizzle with olive oil and sprinkle with salt and pepper. Use your fingers to coat beans evenly with olive oil and spread them out so they don't overlap.
3. Roast in the preheated oven until beans are slightly shriveled and have brown spots, 20 to 25 minutes.

EGG FRIED RICE

Servings: 4 | Prep: 5m | Cooks: 15m | Total: 20m

NUTRITION FACTS

Calories: 145 | Carbohydrates: 24.6g | Fat: 2.7g | Protein: 4.9g | Cholesterol: 46mg

INGREDIENTS

- 1 cup water
- 1/2 teaspoon salt
- 2 tablespoons soy sauce
- 1 cup uncooked instant rice
- 1 teaspoon vegetable oil
- 1/2 onion, finely chopped
- 1/2 cup green beans
- 1 egg, lightly beaten
- 1/4 teaspoon ground black pepper

DIRECTIONS

1. In a saucepan bring water, salt and soy sauce to a boil. Add rice and stir. Remove from heat, cover and let stand 5 minutes.
2. Heat oil in a medium skillet or wok over medium heat. Saute onions and green beans for 2 to 3 minutes. Pour in egg and fry for 2 minutes, scrambling egg while it cooks.
3. Stir in the cooked rice, mix well and sprinkle with pepper.

CHICKEN AND BROCCOLI PASTA

Servings: 8 | Prep: 10m | Cooks: 10m | Total: 20m

NUTRITION FACTS

Calories: 368 | Carbohydrates: 51g | Fat: 7.7g | Protein: 23.5g | Cholesterol: 34mg

INGREDIENTS

- 3 tablespoons olive oil
- 1 pound skinless, boneless chicken breast halves - cut into 1 inch pieces
- 1 tablespoon chopped onion
- 2 cloves garlic, chopped
- 2 (14.5 ounce) cans diced tomatoes
- 2 cups fresh broccoli florets
- salt and pepper to taste
- 1 pinch dried oregano
- 18 ounces dry penne pasta
- 1/4 cup fresh basil leaves, cut into thin strips
- 2 tablespoons grated Parmesan cheese

DIRECTIONS

1. In a large skillet over medium heat, warm oil and add chicken; cook until slightly brown. Add onion and garlic to cook for about 5 minutes or until garlic is golden and onions are translucent.
2. Add tomatoes, broccoli, salt, pepper and oregano; stir well and bring to a boil. Cover and turn down heat to simmer for about 10 minutes.
3. Meanwhile, bring a large pot of lightly salted water to a boil. Add pasta and cook for 8 to 10 minutes or until tender; drain and add back into pot. Pour chicken sauce into pot and mix well.
4. Add basil and toss well; top with Parmesan cheese. Serve.

LEMONY QUINOA

Servings: 6 | Prep: 15m | Cooks: 10m | Total: 25m

NUTRITION FACTS

Calories: 147 | Carbohydrates: 21.4g | Fat: 4.8g | Protein: 5.9g | Cholesterol: 0mg

INGREDIENTS

- 1/4 cup pine nuts
- 1 cup quinoa
- 2 cups water
- sea salt to taste
- 1/4 cup fresh lemon juice
- 2 stalks celery, chopped
- 1/4 red onion, chopped
- 1/4 teaspoon cayenne pepper
- 1/2 teaspoon ground cumin
- 1 bunch fresh parsley, chopped

DIRECTIONS

1. Toast the pine nuts briefly in a dry skillet over medium heat. This will take about 5 minutes, and stir constantly as they will burn easily. Set aside to cool.
2. In a saucepan, combine the quinoa, water and salt. Bring to a boil, then reduce heat to medium and cook until quinoa is tender and water has been absorbed, about 10 minutes. Cool slightly, then fluff with a fork.
3. Transfer the quinoa to a serving bowl and stir in the pine nuts, lemon juice, celery, onion, cayenne pepper, cumin and parsley. Adjust salt and pepper if needed before serving.

FROZEN VEGETABLE STIR-FRY

Servings: 6 | Prep: 5m | Cooks: 5m | Total: 10m

NUTRITION FACTS

Calories: 88 | Carbohydrates: 13.8g | Fat: 2.9g | Protein: 3.5g | Cholesterol: 0mg

INGREDIENTS

- 2 tablespoons soy sauce
- 1 tablespoon brown sugar
- 2 teaspoons garlic powder
- 2 teaspoons peanut butter
- 2 teaspoons olive oil
- 1 (16 ounce) package frozen mixed vegetables

DIRECTIONS

1. Combine soy sauce, brown sugar, garlic powder, and peanut butter in a small bowl.
2. Heat oil in a large skillet over medium heat; cook and stir frozen vegetables until just tender, 5 to 7 minutes. Remove from heat and fold in soy sauce mixture.

SLOW COOKER BALSAMIC CHICKEN

Servings: 6 | Prep: 15m | Cooks: 4h | Total: 4h15m

NUTRITION FACTS

Calories: 200 | Carbohydrates: 17.6g | Fat: 6.8g | Protein: 18.6g | Cholesterol: 43mg

INGREDIENTS

- 2 tablespoons olive oil
- 1 teaspoon dried basil

- 4 skinless, boneless chicken breast halves, or more to taste
- salt and ground black pepper to taste
- 1 onion, thinly sliced
- 4 cloves garlic
- 1 teaspoon dried oregano
- 1 teaspoon dried rosemary
- 1/2 teaspoon dried thyme
- 1/2 cup balsamic vinegar
- 2 (14.5 ounce) cans crushed tomatoes

DIRECTIONS

1. Drizzle olive oil into the slow cooker. Place chicken breasts on top of oil and season each breast with salt and pepper. Top chicken breasts with onion slices, garlic, oregano, basil, rosemary, and thyme. Drizzle balsamic vinegar over seasoned breasts and pour tomatoes on top.
2. Cook in the slow cooker set to High until chicken is no longer pink in the center and the juices run clear, about 4 hours.

ZUCCHINI COOKIES

Servings: 36 | Prep: 15m | Cooks: 10m | Total: 25m

NUTRITION FACTS

Calories: 81 | Carbohydrates: 13.4g | Fat: 2.7g | Protein: 1g | Cholesterol: 5mg

INGREDIENTS

- 1/2 cup margarine, softened
- 1 cup white sugar
- 1 egg
- 1 cup grated zucchini
- 2 cups all-purpose flour
- 1 teaspoon baking soda
- 1/2 teaspoon salt
- 1 teaspoon ground cinnamon
- 1/2 teaspoon ground cloves
- 1 cup raisins

DIRECTIONS

1. In a medium bowl, cream together the margarine and sugar until smooth. Beat in the egg then stir in the zucchini. Combine the flour, baking soda, salt and cinnamon; stir into the zucchini mixture. Mix in raisins. Cover dough and chill for at least 1 hour or overnight.
2. Preheat oven to 375 degrees F (190 degrees C). Grease cookie sheets. Drop dough by teaspoonfuls onto the prepared cookie sheet. Cookies should be about 2 inches apart.
3. Bake for 8 to 10 minutes in the preheated oven until set. Allow cookies to cool slightly on the cookie sheets before removing to wire racks to cool completely.

MY FAVORITE SESAME NOODLES

Servings: 1 | Prep: 10m | Cooks: 15m | Total: 25m

NUTRITION FACTS

Calories: 787 | Carbohydrates: 114.6g | Fat: 26.1g | Protein: 28.3g | Cholesterol: 0mg

INGREDIENTS

- 1/2 (8 ounce) package spaghetti
- 2 tablespoons peanut butter
- 1 tablespoon honey
- 2 tablespoons tamari
- 1 teaspoon Thai chili sauce
- 1 teaspoon sesame oil
- 1 teaspoon ground ginger
- 1 clove garlic, minced
- 1 green onion, chopped
- 2 teaspoons sesame seeds

DIRECTIONS

1. Fill a large pot with lightly salted water and bring to a rolling boil over high heat. Once the water is boiling, stir in the spaghetti, and return to a boil. Cook the pasta uncovered, stirring occasionally, until the pasta has cooked through, but is still firm to the bite, about 12 minutes. Drain well in a colander set in the sink.
2. Melt the peanut butter in a large microwave-safe glass or ceramic bowl, 15 to 20 seconds (depending on your microwave). Whisk the honey, tamari, and chili sauce into the peanut butter, then stir in the sesame oil and ginger. Mix in the garlic and green onions and toss with the spaghetti. Top with the sesame seeds.

GARLIC CHICKEN FRIED BROWN RICE

Servings: 3 | Prep: 20m | Cooks: 15m | Total: 35m

NUTRITION FACTS

Calories: 444 | Carbohydrates: 57.4g | Fat: 12.8g | Protein: 24.3g | Cholesterol: 43mg

INGREDIENTS

- 2 tablespoons vegetable oil, divided
- 8 ounces skinless, boneless chicken breast, cut into strips
- 1/2 red bell pepper, chopped
- 1/2 cup green onion, chopped
- 4 cloves garlic, minced
- 3 cups cooked brown rice
- 2 tablespoons light soy sauce
- 1 tablespoon rice vinegar
- 1 cup frozen peas, thawed

DIRECTIONS

1. Heat 1 tablespoon of vegetable oil in a large skillet set over medium heat. Add the chicken, bell pepper, green onion and garlic. Cook and stir until the chicken is cooked through, about 5 minutes. Remove the chicken to a plate and keep warm.
2. Heat the remaining tablespoon of oil in the same skillet over medium-high heat. Add the rice; cook and stir to heat through. Stir in the soy sauce, rice vinegar and peas, and continue to cook for 1 minute. Return the chicken mixture to the skillet and stir to blend with the rice and heat through before serving.

EASY MASOOR DAAL

Servings: 4 | Prep: 5m | Cooks: 30m | Total: 35m

NUTRITION FACTS

Calories: 185 | Carbohydrates: 25g | Fat: 5.2g | Protein: 11.1g | Cholesterol: 0mg

INGREDIENTS

- 1 cup red lentils
- 1 slice ginger, 1 inch piece, peeled
- 1/2 teaspoon cayenne pepper, or to taste
- 4 teaspoons vegetable oil

- 1/4 teaspoon ground turmeric
- 1 teaspoon salt
- 4 teaspoons dried minced onion
- 1 teaspoon cumin seeds

DIRECTIONS

1. Rinse lentils thoroughly and place in a medium saucepan along with ginger, turmeric, salt and cayenne pepper. Cover with about 1 inch of water and bring to a boil. Skim off any foam that forms on top of the lentils. Reduce heat and simmer, stirring occasionally, until beans are tender and soupy.
2. Meanwhile, in a microwave safe dish combine oil, dried onion and cumin seeds. Microwave on high for 45 seconds to 1 minute; be sure to brown, but not burn, onions. Stir into lentil mixture.

MEXICAN RICE

Servings: 7 | Prep: 15m | Cooks: 30m | Total: 45m

NUTRITION FACTS

Calories: 79 | Carbohydrates: 15.1g | Fat: 1.2g | Protein: 1.5g | Cholesterol: 0mg

INGREDIENTS

- 1 1/2 teaspoons vegetable oil
- 1/2 small small onion, diced
- 2/3 cup uncooked long-grain rice
- 1/2 teaspoon ground cumin
- 1/2 teaspoon chili powder
- 3 ounces canned diced tomatoes
- 1 teaspoon salt
- 1 1/2 cups water

DIRECTIONS

1. In a large saucepan, heat oil over medium heat. Stir in onion and saute until translucent.
2. Pour the rice into the pan and stir to coat grains with oil. Mix in cumin, chili powder, tomatoes, salt and water. Cover, bring to a boil then reduce heat to low. Cook at a simmer for 20 to 30 minutes or until rice is tender. Stir occasionally.

BAKED SCALLOPED POTATOES

Servings: 8 | Prep: 15m | Cooks: 1h15m | Total: 1h30m

NUTRITION FACTS

Calories: 234 | Carbohydrates: 41g | Fat: 3.3g | Protein: 9g | Cholesterol: 3mg

INGREDIENTS

- 6 large peeled, cubed potatoes
- 1 (10.75 ounce) can condensed cream of mushroom soup
- 1 1/4 cups milk
- 1 onion, diced
- 1/2 teaspoon ground black pepper

DIRECTIONS

1. Preheat oven to 375 degrees F (190 degrees C). Grease a 2 quart casserole dish.
2. Layer potatoes and onions into the casserole dish. Combine soup, milk and pepper in a bowl, then pour soup mixture over the potatoes and onions. The soup mixture should almost cover the potatoes and onion, if it does not add extra milk.
3. Cover dish and bake in preheated 375 degrees F (190 degrees C) oven for 60 minutes or until the potatoes are cooked through. At 30 minutes, remove the casserole from the oven and stir once before returning the dish to the oven. Remove from oven and serve.

GOBI ALOO (INDIAN STYLE CAULIFLOWER WITH POTATOES)

Servings: 4 | Prep: 15m | Cooks: 20m | Total: 35m

NUTRITION FACTS

Calories: 135 | Carbohydrates: 23.1g | Fat: 4g | Protein: 4g | Cholesterol: 0mg

INGREDIENTS

- 1 tablespoon vegetable oil
- 1 teaspoon cumin seeds
- 1 teaspoon minced garlic
- 1/2 teaspoon paprika
- 1 teaspoon ground cumin
- 1/2 teaspoon garam masala

- 1 teaspoon ginger paste
- 2 medium potatoes, peeled and cubed
- 1/2 teaspoon ground turmeric
- salt to taste
- 1 pound cauliflower
- 1 teaspoon chopped fresh cilantro

DIRECTIONS

1. Heat the oil in a medium skillet over medium heat. Stir in the cumin seeds, garlic, and ginger paste. Cook about 1 minute until garlic is lightly browned. Add the potatoes. Season with turmeric, paprika, cumin, garam masala, and salt. Cover and continue cooking 5 to 7 minutes stirring occasionally.
2. Mix the cauliflower and cilantro into the saucepan. Reduce heat to low and cover. Stirring occasionally, continue cooking 10 minutes, or until potatoes and cauliflower are tender.

KIKI'S BORRACHO (DRUNKEN) BEANS

Servings: 12 | Prep: 30m | Cooks: 3h | Total: 3h30m

NUTRITION FACTS

Calories: 181 | Carbohydrates: 31.8g | Fat: 1g | Protein: 9.6g | Cholesterol: 0mg

INGREDIENTS

- 1 pound dried pinto beans, washed
- 2 quarts chicken stock
- 1 tablespoon salt
- 1/2 tablespoon ground black pepper
- 1 (12 fluid ounce) can or bottle dark beer
- 2 (14.5 ounce) cans chopped stewed tomatoes
- 1 white onion, diced
- 1/4 cup pickled jalapeno peppers
- 6 cloves garlic, chopped
- 3 bay leaves
- 1 1/2 tablespoons dried oregano
- 1 1/2 cups chopped fresh cilantro

DIRECTIONS

1. Soak beans in a large pot of water overnight.
2. Drain beans, and refill the pot with chicken stock and enough water to cover the beans with 2 inches of liquid. Season with salt and pepper. Cover, and bring to a boil. Reduce heat to medium-low,

cover, and cook for 1 1/2 hours. Stir the beans occasionally through out the entire cooking process to make sure they do not burn or stick to the bottom of the pot.

3. Stir beer, tomatoes, onion, jalapeno peppers, garlic, bay leaves, oregano, and cilantro into the beans. Continue to cook uncovered for 1 hour, or until beans are tender.
4. With a potato masher, crush the beans slightly to thicken the bean liquid. Adjust the seasonings with salt and pepper to taste.

CUBAN BEANS AND RICE

Servings: 6 | Prep: 10m | Cooks: 50m | Total: 1h

NUTRITION FACTS

Calories: 258 | Carbohydrates: 49.3g | Fat: 3.2g | Protein: 7.3g | Cholesterol: 2mg

INGREDIENTS

- 1 tablespoon olive oil
- 1 cup chopped onion
- 1 green bell pepper, chopped
- 2 cloves garlic, minced
- 1 teaspoon salt
- 4 tablespoons tomato paste
- 1 (15.25 ounce) can kidney beans, drained with liquid reserved
- 1 cup uncooked white rice

DIRECTIONS

1. Heat oil in a large saucepan over medium heat. Saute onion, bell pepper and garlic. When onion is translucent add salt and tomato paste. Reduce heat to low and cook 2 minutes. Stir in the beans and rice.
2. Pour the liquid from the beans into a large measuring cup and add enough water to reach a volume of 2 1/2 cups; pour into beans. Cover and cook on low for 45 to 50 minutes, or until liquid is absorbed and rice is cooked.

CILANTRO-LIME RICE

Servings: 6 | Prep: 5m | Cooks: 25m | Total: 30m

NUTRITION FACTS

Calories: 115 | Carbohydrates: 25.2g | Fat: 0.g | Protein: 2.3g | Cholesterol: 1mg

INGREDIENTS

- 1 cup long grain white rice
- 2 cups water
- 1 teaspoon chicken bouillon granules
- 2 tablespoons fresh lime juice
- 2 tablespoons chopped fresh cilantro
- salt to taste

DIRECTIONS

1. Bring the rice, water, and chicken bouillon to a boil in a saucepan over high heat. Reduce heat to medium-low, cover, and simmer until the rice is tender, 20 to 25 minutes. Remove from the heat, add the lime juice, cilantro, and salt; fluff with a fork and serve.
3. Heat the olive oil in a saucepan over low heat; add the green beans to the hot oil and cover the saucepan. Pour the green beans and sauce into the pan and cook, shaking the pan regularly, until the beans are slightly tender, about 5 minutes.

HEALTHIER OVEN ROASTED POTATOES

Servings: 4 | Prep: 15m | Cooks: 20m | Total: 35m

NUTRITION FACTS

Calories: 319 | Carbohydrates: 65.5g | Fat: 3.8g | Protein: 7.7g | Cholesterol: 0mg

INGREDIENTS

- 1 tablespoon olive oil
- 1 tablespoon minced garlic
- 1 tablespoon chopped fresh basil
- 1 tablespoon chopped fresh rosemary
- 1 tablespoon chopped fresh parsley
- 1/2 teaspoon red pepper flakes
- 1/2 teaspoon salt
- 4 large potatoes, peeled and cubed

DIRECTIONS

1. Preheat oven to 475 degrees F (245 degrees C).
2. Combine oil, garlic, basil, rosemary, parsley, red pepper flakes, and salt in a large bowl. Toss in potatoes until evenly coated. Place potatoes in a single layer on a roasting pan or baking sheet.
3. Roast in preheated oven, turning occasionally, until potatoes are brown on all sides, 20 to 30 minutes.

EX-GIRLFRIEND'S MOM'S SALSA FRESCA (PICO DE GALLO)

Servings: 6 | Prep: 20m | Cooks: 20m | Total: 40m | Additional: 20m

NUTRITION FACTS

Calories: 29 | Carbohydrates: 6.9g | Fat: 0.2g | Protein: 1.1g | Cholesterol: 0mg

INGREDIENTS

- 1 cup finely chopped red onion
- 1 jalapeno pepper, seeded and finely chopped - or more to taste
- 2 limes, juiced
- 2 1/2 cups Roma (plum) tomatoes, seeded and chopped
- 1/2 cup chopped fresh cilantro
- 1 teaspoon salt

DIRECTIONS

1. Mix red onion, jalapeno pepper, and lime juice in a bowl. Allow to stand for 5 minutes. Mix in Roma tomatoes, cilantro, and salt; allow to stand 15 more minutes for flavors to blend.

BLACK BEAN SALSA

Servings: 40 | Prep: 15m | Cooks: 8h | Total: 8h15m | Additional: 8h

NUTRITION FACTS

Calories: 42 | Carbohydrates: 8.3g | Fat: 0.2g | Protein: 2.5g | Cholesterol: 0mg

INGREDIENTS

- 3 (15 ounce) cans black beans, drained and rinsed
- 1 (11 ounce) can Mexican-style corn, drained
- 2 (10 ounce) cans diced tomatoes with green chile peppers, partially drained
- 2 tomatoes, diced
- 2 bunches green onions, chopped
- cilantro leaves, for garnish

DIRECTIONS

1. In a large bowl, mix together black beans, Mexican-style corn, diced tomatoes with green chile peppers, tomatoes and green onion stalks. Garnish with desired amount of cilantro leaves. Chill in the refrigerator at least 8 hours, or overnight, before serving.

EASY PASTA FAGIOLI

Servings: 4 | Prep: 10m | Cooks: 30m | Total: 40m

NUTRITION FACTS

Calories: 338 | Carbohydrates: 60.7g | Fat: 5.1g | Protein: 13.4g | Cholesterol: 2mg

INGREDIENTS

- 1 tablespoon olive oil
- 1 carrot, diced
- 1 stalk celery, diced
- 1 thin slice onion, diced
- 1/2 teaspoon chopped garlic
- 4 (8 ounce) cans tomato sauce
- 1 (14 ounce) can chicken broth
- freshly ground black pepper to taste
- 1 tablespoon dried parsley
- 1/2 tablespoon dried basil leaves
- 1 (15 ounce) can cannellini beans, drained and rinsed
- 1 1/2 cups ditalini pasta

DIRECTIONS

1. Heat olive oil in a saucepan over medium heat. Saute carrot, celery and onion until soft. Add garlic and saute briefly. Stir in tomato sauce, chicken broth, pepper, parsley and basil; simmer for 20 minutes.
2. Bring a large pot of lightly salted water to a boil. Add ditalini pasta and cook for 8 minutes or until al dente; drain.
3. Add beans to the sauce mixture and simmer for a few minutes. When pasta is done, stir into sauce and bean mixture.

RESTAURANT-STYLE CHICKEN SCAMPI

Servings: 6 | Prep: 10m | Cooks: 20m | Total: 30m

NUTRITION FACTS

Calories: 548 | Carbohydrates: 74g | Fat: 13.4g | Protein: 31.4g | Cholesterol: 48mg

INGREDIENTS

- 1 pound raw chicken tenders or strips
- 1/4 cup all-purpose flour
- 2 teaspoons olive oil
- 1 (16 ounce) package spaghetti
- 1 teaspoon olive oil
- 1 green bell pepper, cut into 1/2 inch wide strips
- 1 red bell pepper, cut into 1/2 inch wide strips
- 1 yellow bell peppers, cut into 1/2 inch wide strips
- 1 onion, chopped
- 2 tablespoons chopped garlic
- 1 1/2 cups four cheese Alfredo sauce
- 1/2 cup chopped fresh parsley

DIRECTIONS

1. Place chicken and flour in a large resealable plastic bag; seal bag and shake to coat. Heat 2 teaspoons olive oil in a large skillet over medium heat. Shake excess flour off chicken; cook and stir in hot oil for 4 to 5 minutes each side, or until golden brown and cooked through (juices run clear). Remove from skillet and place in a medium bowl; set aside.
2. Bring a large pot of lightly salted water to a boil. Add spaghetti and cook for 8 to 10 minutes or until al dente; drain, reserving 2/3 cup cooking water, and return pasta to pot. Set aside pasta and cooking water.
3. Wipe skillet with paper towel. Heat 1 teaspoon oil in skillet over medium heat. Add green bell pepper, red bell pepper, yellow bell pepper, onion, and garlic and cook and stir for 3 minutes. Cover, reduce heat to low and cook 3 minutes more or until vegetables are tender.
4. Stir in Alfredo sauce, cover and heat for 1 to 2 minutes. Remove from heat and add to reserved pasta in pot, then add reserved cooking water and chicken. Toss to mix, pour into serving bowls and sprinkle with fresh chopped parsley.

LEMON ORZO PRIMAVERA

Servings: 4 | Prep: 15m | Cooks: 15m | Total: 30m

NUTRITION FACTS

Calories: 279 | Carbohydrates: 44.7g | Fat: 6.3g | Protein: 10.4g | Cholesterol: 4mg

INGREDIENTS

- 1 tablespoon olive oil
- 1 (14 ounce) can vegetable broth

- 1 cup uncooked orzo pasta
- 1 clove garlic, crushed
- 1 medium zucchini, shredded
- 1 medium carrot, shredded
- 1 lemon, zested
- 1 tablespoon chopped fresh thyme
- 1/4 cup grated Parmesan cheese

DIRECTIONS

1. Heat the oil in a pot over medium heat. Stir in orzo, and cook 2 minutes, until golden. Stir in garlic, zucchini, and carrot, and cook 2 minutes. Pour in the broth and mix in lemon zest. Bring to a boil. Reduce heat to low and simmer 10 minutes, or until liquid has been absorbed and orzo is tender. Season with thyme and top with Parmesan to serve.

FRUIT SALSA WITH CINNAMON TORTILLA CHIPS

Servings: 32 | Prep: 30m | Cooks: 5m | Total: 1h | Additional: 25m

NUTRITION FACTS

Calories: 70 | Carbohydrates: 12.5g | Fat: 1.8g | Protein: 1.3g | Cholesterol: 0mg

INGREDIENTS

- 1 Fuji apple - peeled, cored and diced
- 1 cup sliced fresh strawberries
- 2 kiwis, peeled and sliced
- 2 bananas, peeled and sliced
- 1 tablespoon fresh lime juice
- 2 tablespoons white sugar
- 1/2 teaspoon ground cinnamon
- 1/2 teaspoon ground nutmeg
- 1 cup oil for frying
- 6 (10 inch) flour tortillas
- 3 tablespoons white sugar
- 1 tablespoon ground cinnamon

DIRECTIONS

1. In a medium bowl, mix together Fuji apple, strawberries, kiwis, bananas, lime juice, white sugar, cinnamon and nutmeg. Cover and chill in the refrigerator approximately 20 minutes.
2. Heat oil in a medium heavy saucepan to 375 degrees F (190 degrees C).

3. Slice flour tortillas into triangles. Carefully place tortilla triangles into the hot oil and fry until golden brown, 2 to 4 minutes. Drain on paper towels.
4. Place white sugar and cinnamon in a large ziplock plastic bag. Drop fried tortilla triangles into the bag and shake to coat.
5. Serve the cinnamon chips warm with the chilled fruit salsa.

BAKED SWEET POTATOES WITH GINGER AND HONEY

Servings: 12 | Prep: 15m | Cooks: 40m | Total: 55m

NUTRITION FACTS

Calories: 162 | Carbohydrates: 34.9g | Fat: 2.3g | Protein: 1.9g | Cholesterol: 0mg

INGREDIENTS

- 3 pounds sweet potatoes, peeled and cubed
- 1/2 cup honey
- 3 tablespoons grated fresh ginger
- 2 tablespoons walnut oil
- 1 teaspoon ground cardamom
- 1/2 teaspoon ground black pepper

DIRECTIONS

1. Preheat oven to 400 degrees F (200 degrees C).
2. In a large bowl, toss together the sweet potatoes, honey, ginger, walnut oil, cardamom, and pepper. Transfer to a large cast iron frying pan.
3. Bake for 20 minutes in the preheated oven. Stir the potatoes to expose the pieces from the bottom of the pan. Bake for another 20 minutes, or until the sweet potatoes are tender and caramelized on the outside.

PUMPKIN PUREE

Servings: 5 | Prep: 30m | Cooks: 1h | Total: 1h30m

NUTRITION FACTS

Calories: 189 | Carbohydrates: 47.2g | Fat: 0.7g | Protein: 7.3g | Cholesterol: 0mg

INGREDIENTS

- 1 sugar pumpkin

DIRECTIONS

1. Preheat oven to 325 degrees F (165 degrees C).
2. Cut the pumpkin in half, stem to base. Remove seeds and pulp. Cover each half with foil.
3. Bake in the preheated oven, foil side up, 1 hour, or until tender.
4. Scrape pumpkin meat from shell halves and puree in a blender. Strain to remove any remaining stringy pieces. Store in the freezer in freezer safe bags.

VEGAN LASAGNA

Servings: 8 | Prep: 30m | Cooks: 2h | Total: 2h30m

NUTRITION FACTS

Calories: 511 | Carbohydrates: 69.9 g | Fat: 15.8g | Protein: 32.5g | Cholesterol: 0mg

INGREDIENTS

- 2 tablespoons olive oil
- 1 1/2 cups chopped onion
- 3 tablespoons minced garlic
- 4 (14.5 ounce) cans stewed tomatoes
- 1/3 cup tomato paste
- 1/2 cup chopped fresh basil
- 1/2 cup chopped parsley
- 1 teaspoon salt
- 1 teaspoon ground black pepper
- 1 (16 ounce) package lasagna noodles
- 2 pounds firm tofu
- 2 tablespoons minced garlic
- 1/4 cup chopped fresh basil
- 1/4 cup chopped parsley
- 1/2 teaspoon salt
- ground black pepper to taste
- 3 (10 ounce) packages frozen chopped spinach, thawed and drained

DIRECTIONS

1. Make the sauce: In a large, heavy saucepan, over medium heat, heat the olive oil. Place the onions in the saucepan and saute them until they are soft, about 5 minutes. Add the garlic; cook 5 minutes more.
2. Place the tomatoes, tomato paste, basil and parsley in the saucepan. Stir well, turn the heat to low and let the sauce simmer covered for 1 hour. Add the salt and pepper.

3. While the sauce is cooking bring a large kettle of salted water to a boil. Boil the lasagna noodles for 9 minutes, then drain and rinse well.
4. Preheat the oven to 400 degrees F (200 degrees C).
5. Place the tofu blocks in a large bowl. Add the garlic, basil and parsley. Add the salt and pepper, and mash all the ingredients together by squeezing pieces of tofu through your fingers. Mix well.
6. Assemble the lasagna: Spread 1 cup of the tomato sauce in the bottom of a 9x13 inch casserole pan. Arrange a single layer of lasagna noodles, sprinkle one-third of the tofu mixture over the noodles. Distribute the spinach evenly over the tofu. Next ladle 1 1/2 cups tomato sauce over the tofu, and top it with another layer of the noodles. Then sprinkle another 1/3 of the tofu mixture over the noodles, top the tofu with 1 1/2 cups tomato sauce, and place a final layer of noodles over the tomato sauce. Finally, top the noodles with the final 1/3 of the tofu, and spread the remaining tomato sauce over everything.

CUBAN BLACK BEANS

Servings: 8 | Prep: 15m | Cooks: 1h30m | Total: 9h45m

NUTRITION FACTS

Calories: 290 | Carbohydrates: 44g | Fat: 7.8g | Protein: 13.8g | Cholesterol: 0mg

INGREDIENTS

- 1 pound black beans, washed
- 1/4 cup olive oil
- 1 large onion, chopped
- 1 medium green bell pepper, chopped
- 6 cloves garlic, peeled and minced
- 5 cups water
- 1 (6 ounce) can tomato paste
- 1 (4 ounce) jar diced pimentos, drained
- 1 tablespoon vinegar
- 2 teaspoons salt
- 1 teaspoon white sugar
- 1 teaspoon black pepper

DIRECTIONS

1. Place beans in a large saucepan with enough water to cover, and soak 8 hours, or overnight; drain.
2. Heat oil in a medium saucepan over medium heat, and saute onion, green bell pepper, and garlic until tender.
3. Into the onion mixture, stir the drained beans, water, tomato paste, pimentos, and vinegar. Season with salt, sugar, and pepper. Bring to a boil. Cover, reduce heat, and simmer 1 1/2 hours, stirring occasionally, until beans are tender.

POTATO AND BEAN ENCHILADAS

Servings: 12 | Prep: 1h | Cooks: 45m | Total: 1h45m

NUTRITION FACTS

Calories: 247 | Carbohydrates: 41.5g | Fat: 5.7g | Protein: 9.5g | Cholesterol: 9mg

INGREDIENTS

- 1 pound potatoes, peeled and diced
- 1 teaspoon cumin
- 1 teaspoon chili powder
- 1 teaspoon salt
- 1 tablespoon ketchup
- 1 pound fresh tomatillos, husks removed
- 1 large onion, chopped
- 1 bunch fresh cilantro, coarsely chopped, divided
- 2 (12 ounce) packages corn tortilla
- 1 (15.5 ounce) can pinto beans, drained
- 1 (12 ounce) package queso fresco
- oil for frying

DIRECTIONS

1. Preheat oven to 400 degrees F (205 degrees C). In a bowl, toss diced potatoes together with cumin, chili powder, salt, and ketchup, and place in an oiled baking dish. Bake in the preheated oven for 20 to 25 minutes, or until tender.
2. Meanwhile, boil tomatillos and chopped onion in water to cover for 10 minutes. Set aside to cool. Once cooled, puree with half of the cilantro until smooth.
3. Fry tortillas individually in a small amount of hot oil until soft.
4. Mix potatoes together with pinto beans, 1/2 cheese, and 1/2 cilantro. Fill tortillas with potato mixture, and roll up. Place seam side down in an oiled 9x13 inch baking dish. Spoon tomatillo sauce over enchiladas, and spread remaining cheese over sauce. Bake for 20 minutes, or until hot and bubbly.

THAI SPICY BASIL CHICKEN FRIED RICE

Servings: 6 | Prep: 30m | Cooks: 10m | Total: 40m

NUTRITION FACTS

Calories: 794 | Carbohydrates: 116.4g | Fat: 22.1g | Protein: 29.1g | Cholesterol: 46mg

INGREDIENTS

- 3 tablespoons oyster sauce
- 2 tablespoons fish sauce
- 1 teaspoon white sugar
- 1/2 cup peanut oil for frying
- 4 cups cooked jasmine rice, chilled
- 6 large cloves garlic clove, crushed
- 2 serrano peppers, crushed
- 1 pound boneless, skinless chicken breast, cut into thin strips
- 1 red pepper, seeded and thinly sliced
- 1 onion, thinly sliced
- 2 cups sweet Thai basil
- 1 cucumber, sliced (optional)
- 1/2 cup cilantro sprigs (optional)

DIRECTIONS

1. Whisk together the oyster sauce, fish sauce, and sugar in a bowl.
2. Heat the oil in a wok over medium-high heat until the oil begins to smoke. Add the garlic and serrano peppers, stirring quickly. Stir in the chicken, bell pepper, onion and oyster sauce mixture; cook until the chicken is no longer pink. Raise heat to high and stir in the chilled rice; stir quickly until the sauce is blended with the rice. Use the back of a spoon to break up any rice sticking together.
3. Remove from heat and mix in the basil leaves. Garnish with sliced cucumber and cilantro as desired.

CAVATELLI AND BROCCOLI

Servings: 12 | Prep: 10m | Cooks: 25m | Total: 35m

NUTRITION FACTS

Calories: 317 | Carbohydrates: 47.6g | Fat: 10.3g | Protein: 10.2g | Cholesterol: 1mg

INGREDIENTS

- 3 heads fresh broccoli, cut into florets
- 1/2 cup olive oil
- 3 cloves garlic, minced
- 1 teaspoon salt
- 1 teaspoon crushed red pepper flakes
- 2 tablespoons grated Parmesan cheese

- 1 1/2 pounds cavatelli pasta

DIRECTIONS

1. In a large pot of boiling water, blanch broccoli for about 5 minutes. Drain, and set aside.
2. Heat olive oil in a large skillet over medium heat. Saute garlic until lightly golden, being careful not to burn it. Add the broccoli. Saute, stirring occasionally, for about 10 minutes. Broccoli should be tender yet crisp to the bite.
3. Meanwhile, cook cavatelli in a large pot of boiling salted water for 8 to 10 minutes, or until al dente. Drain, and place in a large serving bowl. Toss with the broccoli, and season with salt and hot pepper flakes. Serve with parmesan cheese.

ALBINO PASTA

Servings: 8 | Prep: 15m | Cooks: 10m | Total: 25m

NUTRITION FACTS

Calories: 275 | Carbohydrates: 41g | Fat: 9g | Protein: 8.8g | Cholesterol: 3mg

INGREDIENTS

- 1 (16 ounce) package dry penne pasta
- 4 tablespoons olive oil
- 1 teaspoon minced garlic
- 1/3 cup grated Parmesan cheese

DIRECTIONS

1. Bring a large pot of lightly salted water to a boil. Add penne pasta and cook for 8 to 10 minutes or until al dente; drain.
2. In small saucepan, saute garlic a small amount of oil. Combine garlic, olive oil, and pasta in a bowl. Mix in parmesan cheese.

PASTA HOT! HOT! HOT!

Servings: 4 | Prep: 15m | Cooks: 15m | Total: 30m

NUTRITION FACTS

Calories: 561 | Carbohydrates: 84.8g | Fat: 16.7g | Protein: 16.7g | Cholesterol: 4mg

INGREDIENTS

- 1 (16 ounce) package spaghetti
- 1/4 cup olive oil
- 3 cloves garlic, chopped
- 1/2 teaspoon crushed red pepper
- 1/4 cup grated Parmesan cheese

DIRECTIONS

1. Bring a large pot of lightly salted water to a boil. Add pasta and cook for 8 to 10 minutes or until al dente; drain.
2. In a small saucepan over low heat place olive oil, garlic and peppers and simmer. Pour olive oil mixture over cooked pasta and serve with Parmesan cheese.

RICE WITH BLACK BEANS

Servings: 8 | Prep: 5m | Cooks: 15m | Total: 20m

NUTRITION FACTS

Calories: 80 | Carbohydrates: 14.4g | Fat: 2g | Protein: 1.6g | Cholesterol: 0mg

INGREDIENTS

- 1 onion, chopped
- 1 tablespoon vegetable oil
- 1 (14.5 ounce) can stewed tomatoes
- 1 (15 ounce) can black beans, undrained
- 1/2 teaspoon dried oregano
- 1/2 teaspoon garlic powder
- 1 cup instant white rice

DIRECTIONS

1. In a large saucepan, cook and stir onion in oil until tender and translucent, but not brown. Add tomatoes, beans, oregano and garlic powder. Bring to boil. Stir in rice, return mixture to a boil. Reduce heat to simmer, and cover.
2. Let mixture simmer for 5 minutes. Remove pan from heat and let stand 5 minutes before serving.

CINNAMON AND LIME CHICKEN FAJITAS

Servings: 6 | Prep: 15m | Cooks: 40m | Total: 55m

NUTRITION FACTS

Calories: 395 | Carbohydrates: 49.5g | Fat: 12.9g | Protein: 22.3g | Cholesterol: 45mg

INGREDIENTS

- 4 boneless, skinless chicken breast halves
- 1 tablespoon ground cinnamon
- salt and pepper to taste
- 2 large baking potatoes, peeled and cubed
- ¼ cup canola oil
- 1 large yellow onion, chopped
- 1 large clove garlic, peeled and minced
- 1 tablespoon chopped jalapeno peppers
- 1 lime, juiced
- 12 (6 inch) corn tortillas, warmed

DIRECTIONS

1. Preheat oven to 400 degrees F (200 degrees C).
2. Place potatoes in a shallow baking dish. Drizzle with about 1/2 the oil, and season with salt. Bake 30 to 40 minutes in the preheated oven, until tender.
3. Meanwhile, season chicken with cinnamon, salt, and pepper. Arrange in a separate baking dish, and bake 30 minutes in the preheated oven, until no longer pink and juices run clear. Cool and shred.
4. Heat remaining oil in a skillet over medium heat, and saute onion and garlic until tender. Mix in shredded chicken, jalapeno, and lime juice. Cook until heated through.
5. Serve the chicken and potatoes in warmed tortillas.

HARD CANDY

Servings: 36 | Prep: 5m | Cooks: 25m | Total: 45m

NUTRITION FACTS

Calories: 124 | Carbohydrates: 32.2g | Fat: 0g | Protein: 0g | Cholesterol: 0mg

INGREDIENTS

- 3 3/4 cups white sugar
- 1 1/2 cups light corn
- 1 tablespoon orange, or other flavored extract
- 1/2 teaspoon food coloring

- syrup
- 1 cup water
- (optional)
- 1/4 cup confectioners' sugar for dusting

DIRECTIONS

1. In a medium saucepan, stir together the white sugar, corn syrup, and water. Cook, stirring, over medium heat until sugar dissolves, then bring to a boil. Without stirring, heat to 300 to 310 degrees F (149 to 154 degrees C), or until a small amount of syrup dropped into cold water forms hard, brittle threads.
2. Remove from heat and stir in flavored extract and food coloring, if desired. Pour onto a greased cookie sheet, and dust the top with confectioners' sugar. Let cool, and break into pieces. Store in an airtight container.

QUINOA BREAKFAST PUDDING

Servings: 6 | Prep: 5m | Cooks: 35m | Total: 40m

NUTRITION FACTS

Calories: 202 | Carbohydrates: 42.6g | Fat: 1.9g | Protein: 4.4g | Cholesterol: 0mg

INGREDIENTS

- 1 cup quinoa
- 2 cups water
- 2 cups apple juice
- 1 cup raisins
- 2 tablespoons lemon juice
- 1 teaspoon ground cinnamon, or to taste
- salt to taste
- 2 teaspoons vanilla extract

DIRECTIONS

1. Place quinoa in a sieve and rinse thoroughly. Allow to drain, then place quinoa in a medium saucepan with water. Bring to a boil over high heat. Cover pan with lid, lower heat, and allow to simmer until all water is absorbed and quinoa is tender, about 15 minutes.
2. Mix in apple juice, raisins, lemon juice, cinnamon, and salt. Cover pan and allow to simmer for 15 minutes longer. Stir in vanilla extract. Serve warm.

ROASTED VEGETABLE ORZO

Servings: 4 | Prep: 25m | Cooks: 20m | Total: 45m

NUTRITION FACTS

Calories: 621 | Carbohydrates: 104.5g | Fat: 11.4g | Protein: 24.9g | Cholesterol: 3mg

INGREDIENTS

- 1 zucchini, sliced
- 1 summer squash, sliced
- 1 red onion, cut into chunks
- 1 pound asparagus, cut into 1-inch pieces
- 1 pound portobello mushrooms, thickly sliced
- 4 cloves garlic, minced
- 2 tablespoons olive oil
- 1 pinch white sugar
- salt and black pepper to taste
- 4 cubes chicken bouillon
- 1/4 cup dry white wine
- 1 (16 ounce) package orzo pasta
- 2 tablespoons grated Parmesan cheese

DIRECTIONS

1. Preheat oven to 450 degrees F (230 degrees C).
2. Place the zucchini, squash, onion, asparagus, and mushrooms in a large bowl; add in garlic, olive oil and sugar, and stir gently to coat vegetables. Spread vegetables in a single layer on a baking sheet, and sprinkle with salt and pepper.
3. Roast vegetables until tender, 20 to 25 minutes.
4. Meanwhile, bring a large pot of lightly salted water to boil. Add bouillon cubes, wine, and orzo, and cook until al dente, about 8 to 10 minutes. Drain. Stir in roasted vegetables and Parmesan cheese, and serve warm.

PESTO PASTA

Servings: 8 | Prep: 5m | Cooks: 10m | Total: 15m

NUTRITION FACTS

Calories: 225 | Carbohydrates: 32g | Fat: 7.2g | Protein: 7.8g | Cholesterol: 44mg

INGREDIENTS

- 1/2 cup chopped onion
- 2 1/2 tablespoons pesto
- 2 tablespoons olive oil
- 2 tablespoons grated Parmesan cheese
- 1 (16 ounce) package pasta
- salt to taste
- ground black pepper to taste

DIRECTIONS

1. Cook pasta in a large pot of boiling water until done. Drain.
2. Meanwhile, heat the oil in a frying pan over medium low heat. Add pesto, onion, and salt and pepper. Cook about five minutes, or until onions are soft.
3. In a large bowl, mix pesto mixture into pasta. Stir in grated cheese. Serve.

MIKE'S HOMEMADE PIZZA

Servings: 8 | Prep: 1h10m | Cooks: 20m | Total: 1h30m

NUTRITION FACTS

Calories: 239 | Carbohydrates: 41.3g | Fat: 5.6g | Protein: 6.2g | Cholesterol: 0mg

INGREDIENTS

- 1 (.25 ounce) envelope active dry yeast
- 1 cup lukewarm water
- 3 cups all-purpose flour
- 1/4 teaspoon salt
- 2 tablespoons shortening
- 1 tablespoon vegetable oil
- 1/2 cup chopped onion
- 1 (6 ounce) can tomato paste
- 6 fluid ounces water
- 1/2 teaspoon white sugar
- 1 teaspoon salt
- 1/8 teaspoon ground black pepper
- 1/4 teaspoon garlic powder
- 1/4 teaspoon dried basil
- 1/2 teaspoon dried oregano
- 1/4 teaspoon dried marjoram
- 1/4 teaspoon ground cumin
- 1/4 teaspoon chili powder
- 1/8 teaspoon crushed red pepper flakes

DIRECTIONS

1. In a small bowl, dissolve yeast in warm water. Let stand until creamy, about 10 minutes.
2. In a large bowl, combine flour, salt and shortening. Stir in the yeast mixture. When the dough has pulled together, turn it out onto a lightly floured surface, and knead until smooth and elastic, about 8 minutes. Lightly oil a large bowl, place the dough in the bowl, and turn to coat with oil. Cover with a damp cloth, and let rise in a warm place until doubled in volume, about 45 minutes.
3. Heat oil in a small saucepan over medium heat. Saute onion until tender. Stir in tomato paste and water. Season with sugar, salt, black pepper, garlic powder, basil, oregano, marjoram, cumin, chili powder and red pepper flakes. Simmer 15 to 20 minutes.
4. Recipe makes 2 (12 inch) pizzas. Divide dough in half, and spread onto pizza pans. Cover with sauce, and desired toppings. Bake at 400 degrees for 20 minutes, or until crust is golden brown.

EASY LIMA BEANS

Servings: 6 | Prep: 15m | Cooks: 30m | Total: 45m

NUTRITION FACTS

Calories: 84 | Carbohydrates: 15.9g | Fat: 0g | Protein: 4.1g | Cholesterol: 0mg

INGREDIENTS

- cooking spray
- 1/2 medium onion, finely chopped
- 1 1/2 cups chicken broth
- 1 (16 ounce) package frozen baby lima beans

DIRECTIONS

1. Heat a large saucepan over medium heat, and spray with cooking spray. Saute onions until soft and translucent. Pour in chicken broth, and bring to a boil. Add lima beans, and enough water just to cover. Bring to a boil, then reduce heat to low, cover, and simmer for 30 minutes, until beans are tender.

DOREEN'S HAM SLICES ON THE GRILL

Servings: 4 | Prep: 10m | Cooks: 15m | Total: 25m

NUTRITION FACTS

Calories: 245 | Carbohydrates: 58g | Fat: 1.3g | Protein: 2.7g | Cholesterol: 8mg

INGREDIENTS

- 1 cup packed brown sugar
- 1/3 cup prepared horseradish
- 1/4 cup lemon juice
- 2 slices ham

DIRECTIONS

1. Preheat an outdoor grill for high heat and lightly oil grate.
2. In a small bowl, mix brown sugar, lemon juice and prepared horseradish.
3. Heat the brown sugar mixture in the microwave on high heat 1 minute, or until warm.
4. Score both sides of ham slices. Place on the prepared grill. Baste continuously with the brown sugar mixture while grilling. Grill 6 to 8 minutes per side, or to desired doneness.

BROKEN SPAGHETTI RISOTTO

Servings: 2 | Prep: 10m | Cooks: 15m | Total: 25m

NUTRITION FACTS

Calories: 518 | Carbohydrates: 86.3g | Fat: 10.5g | Protein: 17.8g | Cholesterol: 9mg

INGREDIENTS

- 1 tablespoon olive oil
- 1/2 teaspoon red pepper flakes, or to taste
- 8 ounces uncooked spaghetti, broken into 1 inch pieces
- salt to taste
- 2 cloves garlic, minced
- 2 tablespoons freshly grated Parmigiano-Reggiano cheese, or to taste
- 1 1/2 cups chicken broth
- 1 tablespoon chopped fresh flat-leaf parsley

DIRECTIONS

1. Heat oil in a saucepan over medium heat; add spaghetti and toast, stirring constantly, until golden brown, 3 to 5 minutes.
2. Stir garlic into spaghetti pieces and cook for 30 seconds.

3. Pour in 1/2 cup broth and increase heat to medium high. Stir spaghetti and broth until all the liquid is absorbed, 2 to 3 minutes. Repeat this process until all of the stock is absorbed and noodles are desired tenderness, about 10 minutes.
4. Reduce heat to low. Season spaghetti with salt and red pepper flakes to taste. Remove from heat.
5. Stir Parmigiano-Reggiano cheese and parsley into spaghetti and serve.

EASY LIMA BEANS

Servings: 6 | Prep: 15m | Cooks: 30m | Total: 45m

NUTRITION FACTS

Calories: 84 | Carbohydrates: 15.9g | Fat: 0g | Protein: 4.1g | Cholesterol: 0mg

INGREDIENTS

- cooking spray
- 1/2 medium onion, finely chopped
- 1 1/2 cups chicken broth
- 1 (16 ounce) package frozen baby lima beans

DIRECTIONS

1. Heat a large saucepan over medium heat, and spray with cooking spray. Saute onions until soft and translucent. Pour in chicken broth, and bring to a boil. Add lima beans, and enough water just to cover. Bring to a boil, then reduce heat to low, cover, and simmer for 30 minutes, until beans are tender.

CHICKEN YAKISOBA

Servings: 4 | Prep: 20m | Cooks: 15m | Total: 35m

NUTRITION FACTS

Calories: 503 | Carbohydrates: 69.8g | Fat: 16.5g | Protein: 26.5g | Cholesterol: 29mg

INGREDIENTS

- 2 tablespoons canola oil
- 1 tablespoon sesame oil
- 2 skinless, boneless chicken breast halves - cut into bite-size pieces
- 1/2 medium head cabbage, thinly sliced
- 1 onion, sliced
- 2 carrots, cut into matchsticks

- 2 cloves garlic, minced
- 2 tablespoons Asian-style chile paste
- 1/2 cup soy sauce
- 1 tablespoon canola oil
- 1 tablespoon salt
- 2 pounds cooked yakisoba noodles
- 2 tablespoons pickled ginger, or to taste (optional)

DIRECTIONS

1. Heat 2 tablespoons canola oil and sesame oil in a large skillet over medium-high heat. Cook and stir chicken and garlic in hot oil until fragrant, about 1 minute. Stir chile paste into chicken mixture; cook and stir until chicken is completely browned, 3 to 4 minutes. Add soy sauce and simmer for 2 minutes. Pour chicken and sauce into a bowl.
2. Heat 1 tablespoon canola oil in the skillet over medium-high heat; cook and stir cabbage, onion, carrots, and salt in hot oil until cabbage is wilted, 3 to 4 minutes.
3. Stir the chicken mixture into the cabbage mixture. Add noodles; cook and stir until noodles are hot and chicken is no longer pink inside, 3 to 4 minutes. Garnish with pickled ginger.

ZUCCHINI WITH CHICKPEA AND MUSHROOM STUFFING

Servings: 8 | Prep: 30m | Cooks: 30m | Total: 1h

NUTRITION FACTS

Calories: 107 | Carbohydrates: 18.4g | Fat: 2.7g | Protein: 4.5g | Cholesterol: 0mg

INGREDIENTS

- 4 zucchini, halved
- 1 tablespoon olive oil
- 1 onion, chopped
- 2 cloves garlic, crushed
- 1/2 (8 ounce) package button mushrooms, sliced
- 1 teaspoon ground coriander
- 1 1/2 teaspoons ground cumin, or to taste
- 1 (15.5 ounce) can chickpeas, rinsed and drained
- 1/2 lemon, juiced
- 2 tablespoons chopped fresh parsley
- sea salt to taste
- ground black pepper to taste

DIRECTIONS

1. Preheat oven to 350 degrees F (175 degrees C). Grease a shallow baking dish.
2. Scoop out the flesh of the zucchini; chop the flesh and set aside. Place the shells in the prepared dish.
3. Heat oil in a large skillet over medium heat. Saute onions for 5 minutes, then add garlic and saute 2 minutes more. Stir in chopped zucchini and mushrooms; saute 5 minutes. Stir in coriander, cumin, chickpeas, lemon juice, parsley, salt and pepper. Spoon mixture into zucchini shells.
4. Bake in preheated oven for 30 to 40 minutes, or until zucchini are tender.

LENTIL RICE AND VEGGIE BAKE

Servings: 6 | Prep: 15m | Cooks: 1h | Total: 1h15m

NUTRITION FACTS

Calories: 187 | Carbohydrates: 35.1g | Fat: 1.5g | Protein: 9.7g | Cholesterol: 0mg

INGREDIENTS

- 1/2 cup uncooked long grain white rice
- 2 1/2 cups water
- 1 cup red lentils
- 1 teaspoon vegetable oil
- 1 small onion, chopped
- 3 cloves garlic, minced
- 1 fresh tomato, chopped
- 1/3 cup chopped celery
- 1/3 cup chopped carrots
- 1/3 cup chopped zucchini
- 1 (8 ounce) can tomato sauce
- 1 teaspoon dried basil
- 1 teaspoon dried oregano
- 1 teaspoon ground cumin
- salt and pepper to taste

DIRECTIONS

1. Place the rice and 1 cup water in a pot, and bring to a boil. Cover, reduce heat to low, and simmer 20 minutes. Place lentils in a pot with the remaining 1 1/2 cups water, and bring to a boil. Cook 15 minutes, or until tender.
2. Preheat oven to 350 degrees F (175 degrees C).
3. Heat the oil in a skillet over medium heat, and stir in the onion and garlic. Mix in tomato, celery, carrots, zucchini, and 1/2 the tomato sauce. Season with 1/2 the basil, 1/2 the oregano, 1/2 the cumin, salt, and pepper. Cook until vegetables are tender.

4. In a casserole dish, mix the rice, lentils, and vegetables. Top with remaining tomato sauce, and sprinkle with remaining basil, oregano, and cumin.
5. Bake 30 minutes in the preheated oven, until bubbly.

MEXICAN QUINOA

Servings: 4 | Prep: 20m | Cooks: 20m | Total: 40m

NUTRITION FACTS

Calories: 244 | Carbohydrates: 38.1g | Fat: 6.1g | Protein: 8.1g | Cholesterol: 2mg

INGREDIENTS

- 1 tablespoon olive oil
- 1 cup quinoa, rinsed
- 1 small onion, chopped
- 2 cloves garlic, minced
- 1 jalapeno pepper, seeded and chopped (optional)
- 1 (10 ounce) can diced tomatoes with green chile peppers (such as RO*TEL®)
- 1 envelope gluten-free taco seasoning mix
- 2 cups low-sodium chicken broth
- 1/4 cup chopped fresh cilantro

DIRECTIONS

1. Heat olive oil in a large skillet over medium heat; cook and stir quinoa and onion in the hot oil until onion is translucent, about 5 minutes. Add garlic and jalapeno pepper to quinoa mixture and cook until garlic is fragrant and slightly softened, 1 or 2 more minutes.
2. Mix undrained can of diced tomatoes with green chiles, taco seasoning mix, and chicken broth into quinoa mixture. Bring to a boil, reduce heat to medium-low, and simmer until liquid has been absorbed, 15 to 20 minutes. Stir in cilantro.

HONEY SOY TILAPIA

Servings: 2 | Prep: 10m | Cooks: 15m | Total: 55m

NUTRITION FACTS

Calories: 218 | Carbohydrates: 33.3g | Fat: 1.4g | Protein: 19.4g | Cholesterol: 31mg

INGREDIENTS

- 3 tablespoons honey
- 3 tablespoons soy sauce
- 3 tablespoons balsamic vinegar
- 1 tablespoon minced garlic
- 2 (3 ounce) fillets tilapia
- cooking spray
- 1 teaspoon freshly cracked black pepper

DIRECTIONS

1. Mix the honey, soy sauce, balsamic vinegar, and garlic together in a bowl. Place the tilapia fillets in the mixture; allow to marinate in refrigerator at least 30 minutes.
2. Preheat an oven to 350 degrees F (175 degrees C). Spray a baking dish with cooking spray.
3. Remove tilapia from marinade, and discard the marinade. Place fillets into the prepared baking sheet, and sprinkle the black pepper over the fish.
4. Bake in the preheated oven until the fish flakes easily with a fork, 15 to 20 minutes.

SPICY MANGO SWEET POTATO CHICKEN

Servings: 5 | Prep: 30m | Cooks: 20m | Total: 50m

NUTRITION FACTS

Calories: 268 | Carbohydrates: 30.2g | Fat: 7.5g | Protein: 21.1g | Cholesterol: 47mg

INGREDIENTS

- 2 cups cubed peeled sweet potatoes
- 2 tablespoons vegetable oil
- 1 pound skinless, boneless chicken breast halves - cubed
- 1 clove garlic, minced
- 6 tablespoons tamari soy sauce
- 3/4 cup water
- 3 tablespoons honey
- 3 tablespoons hot sauce, or to taste
- 1 ripe mango, peeled and cubed
- 1/4 teaspoon crushed red pepper flakes
- 1 teaspoon cornstarch
- 1 tablespoon warm water

DIRECTIONS

1. Place the sweet potatoes into a saucepan and fill with enough water to cover. Simmer over medium-high heat until tender, about 15 minutes. Drain and set aside.
2. Meanwhile, heat 2 tablespoons of vegetable oil in a skillet over medium-high heat. Stir in chicken, and cook until no longer pink in the center, about 5 minutes; set aside. Stir garlic into the skillet, and cook for a few minutes, until fragrant. Pour in the tamari, 3/4 cup of water, honey, and hot sauce. Bring to a simmer, then stir in the sweet potato, chicken, mango, and red pepper flakes. Cook and stir until hot. Dissolve the cornstarch in 1 tablespoon of water, and stir into the simmering mixture; stir until thickened.

SIMPLE BAKED BEANS

Servings: 10 | Prep: 15m | Cooks: 3h | Total: 3h15m

NUTRITION FACTS

Calories: 176 | Carbohydrates: 31.7g | Fat: 3.9g | Protein: 5.6g | Cholesterol: 10mg

INGREDIENTS

- 2 (16 ounce) cans baked beans with pork
- 1/4 cup molasses
- 1/4 cup chopped onions
- 4 tablespoons brown sugar
- 1 tablespoon prepared mustard
- 2 tablespoons ketchup
- 2 slices bacon, chopped

DIRECTIONS

1. Preheat oven to 350 degrees F (175 degrees C).
2. Mix baked beans with pork, molasses, onions, brown sugar and ketchup together and put in a greased casserole dish. Top with bacon, cover and bake for 3 hours or until thick.

FRIED ZUCCHINI

Servings: 4 | Prep: 20m | Cooks: 20m | Total: 40m

NUTRITION FACTS

Calories: 195 | Carbohydrates: 31.1g | Fat: 6.2g | Protein: 4.4g | Cholesterol: 0mg

INGREDIENTS

- 2 zucchini, quartered and sliced
- 1 onion, sliced into rings
- 1/2 cup all-purpose flour
- 1/2 cup cornmeal
- 1/2 teaspoon salt
- 1/2 teaspoon ground black pepper
- 1/4 teaspoon garlic powder
- 1 cup vegetable oil for frying

DIRECTIONS

1. Place zucchini and onions in a medium bowl and mix together.
2. In a small bowl mix flour, cornmeal, salt, pepper and garlic powder.
3. Pour dry mixture over zucchini/onion mixture, cover bowl and shake well. Let mixture sit for about 30 minutes; a batter will form on the vegetables.
4. In a medium skillet heat oil over medium heat. When oil is hot add breaded vegetables and fry, turning to brown evenly.

SALSA DE TOMATILLO

Servings: 16 | Prep: 20m | Cooks: 10m | Total: 30m

NUTRITION FACTS

Calories: 10 | Carbohydrates: 2g | Fat: 0.2g | Protein: 0.3g | Cholesterol: 0mg

INGREDIENTS

- 10 tomatillos, husked
- 1 small onion, chopped
- 3 cloves garlic, chopped
- 2 jalapeno peppers, chopped
- 1/4 cup chopped fresh cilantro
- salt and pepper to taste

DIRECTIONS

1. Place tomatillos in a nonreactive saucepan with enough water to cover. Bring to a boil. Simmer until tomatillos soften and begin to burst, about 10 minutes.
2. Drain tomatillos and place in a food processor or blender with onion, garlic, jalapeno peppers, cilantro, salt and pepper. Blend to desired consistency.

SWEET CHILI THAI SAUCE

Servings: 24 | Prep: 15m | Cooks: 5m | Total: 20m

NUTRITION FACTS

Calories: 34 | Carbohydrates: 8.7g | Fat: 0g | Protein: 0g | Cholesterol: 0mg

INGREDIENTS

- 1 cup water
- 1 cup rice vinegar
- 1 cup sugar
- 2 teaspoons fresh ginger root, minced
- 1 teaspoon garlic, minced
- 2 teaspoons hot chile pepper, minced
- 2 teaspoons ketchup
- 2 teaspoons cornstarch

DIRECTIONS

1. Pour water and vinegar into a saucepan, and bring to a boil over high heat. Stir in sugar, ginger, garlic, chile pepper, and ketchup; simmer for 5 minutes. Stir in cornstarch. Remove saucepan from stove to cool. Then transfer to a bowl, cover, and refrigerate until needed.

SPINACH, RED LENTIL, AND BEAN CURRY

Servings: 4 | Prep: 25m | Cooks: 10m | Total: 35m

NUTRITION FACTS

Calories: 328 | Carbohydrates: 51.9g | Fat: 8.3g | Protein: 18g | Cholesterol: 2mg

INGREDIENTS

- 1 cup red lentils
- 1/4 cup tomato puree
- 1/2 (8 ounce) container plain yogurt
- 1 teaspoon garam masala
- 1/2 teaspoon ground dried turmeric
- 1/2 teaspoon ground cumin
- 1 onion, chopped
- 2 cloves garlic, chopped
- 1 (1 inch) piece fresh ginger root, grated
- 4 cups loosely packed fresh spinach, coarsely chopped
- 2 tomatoes, chopped
- 4 sprigs fresh cilantro,

- chopped
- 1/2 teaspoon ancho chile powder
- 2 tablespoons vegetable oil
- 1 (15.5 ounce) can mixed beans, rinsed and drained

DIRECTIONS

1. Rinse lentils and place in a saucepan with enough water to cover. Bring to a boil. Reduce heat to low, cover pot, and simmer over low heat for 20 minutes. Drain.
2. In a bowl, stir together tomato puree and yogurt. Season with garam masala, turmeric, cumin, and chile powder. Stir until creamy.
3. Heat oil in a skillet over medium heat. Stir in onion, garlic, and ginger; cook until onion begins to brown. Stir in spinach; cook until dark green and wilted. Gradually stir in yogurt mixture. Then mix in tomatoes and cilantro.
4. Stir lentils and mixed beans into mixture until well combined. Heat through, about 5 minutes.

QUICK SESAME GREEN BEANS

Servings: 4 | Prep: 10m | Cooks: 5m | Total: 15m

NUTRITION FACTS

Calories: 45 | Carbohydrates: 7.1g | Fat: 1.4g | Protein: 2.3g | Cholesterol: 0mg

INGREDIENTS

- 8 ounces fresh green beans, trimmed
- 2 tablespoons low sodium soy sauce
- 1/2 tablespoon miso paste
- 1/2 teaspoon red pepper flakes
- 4 cloves garlic, minced
- 1 teaspoon grated fresh ginger root
- 1 tablespoon sesame seeds, toasted

DIRECTIONS

1. Place the green beans into a steamer insert and set in a pot over one inch of water. Bring to a boil, cover and steam for 5 minutes. Remove from the heat and transfer beans to a serving bowl.
2. Meanwhile, in a small bowl, stir together the soy sauce, miso paste, red pepper flakes, garlic and ginger. Pour over the green beans and toss to coat. Sprinkle sesame seeds on top.

EMILY'S FAMOUS MARSHMALLOWS

Servings: 18 | Prep: 30m | Cooks: 20m | Total: 8h40m

NUTRITION FACTS

Calories: 118 | Carbohydrates: 29.8g | Fat: 0g | Protein: 0.4g | Cholesterol: 0mg

INGREDIENTS

- 1 cup confectioners' sugar for dusting
- 2 cups white sugar
- 1 tablespoon light corn syrup
- 1 1/4 cups water, divided
- 4 tablespoons unflavored gelatin
- 2 egg whites
- 1 teaspoon vanilla extract

DIRECTIONS

1. Dust a 9x9 inch square dish generously with confectioners' sugar.
2. In a small saucepan over medium-high heat, stir together white sugar, corn syrup and 3/4 cup water. Heat to 250 to 265 degrees F (121 to 129 degrees C), or until a small amount of syrup dropped into cold water forms a rigid ball. • While syrup is heating, place remaining water in a metal bowl and sprinkle gelatin over the surface. Place bowl over simmering water until gelatin has dissolved completely. Keep in a warm place until syrup has come to temperature. Remove syrup from heat and whisk gelatin mixture into hot syrup. Set aside.
3. In a separate bowl, whip egg whites to soft peaks. Continue to beat, pouring syrup mixture into egg whites in a thin stream, until the egg whites are very stiff. Stir in vanilla. Spread evenly in prepared pan and let rest 8 hours or overnight before cutting.

PINTO BEANS WITH MEXICAN-STYLE SEASONINGS

Servings: 8 | Prep: 15m | Cooks: 4h | Total: 12h15m | Additional: 8h

NUTRITION FACTS

Calories: 267 | Carbohydrates: 40.9g | Fat: 5.2g | Protein: 16.4g | Cholesterol: 10mg

INGREDIENTS

- 1 pound dried pinto beans, rinsed
- 2 (10 ounce) cans diced tomatoes with green
- 1 tablespoon ground cumin, or to taste
- 1 1/2 teaspoons garlic powder, or to taste

chile peppers (such as RO*TEL®)
- 1/2 pound bacon, cut into 1/2-inch pieces
- 1 yellow onion, chopped
- 1 tablespoon chili powder, or to taste
- 1/2 bunch fresh cilantro, chopped
- salt to taste

DIRECTIONS

1. Place pinto beans into a large pot and pour in enough water to cover by 2 to 3 inches. Let beans soak overnight.
2. Drain beans, return to pot, and pour in fresh water to cover; add diced tomatoes, bacon, onion, chili powder, cumin, and garlic powder. Bring to a boil, reduce heat to low, and simmer for 3 hours.
3. Stir cilantro and salt into bean mixture; simmer until beans are soft, about 1 more hour.

GRILLED BAKED POTATOES

Servings: 6 | Prep: 5m | Cooks: 25m | Total: 30m

NUTRITION FACTS

Calories: 194 | Carbohydrates: 35.8g | Fat: 4.7g | Protein: 1.6g | Cholesterol: 0mg

INGREDIENTS

- 4 large baking potatoes, quartered
- 2 tablespoons olive oil
- 2 teaspoons freshly ground black pepper
- 2 teaspoons garlic powder
- 2 teaspoons dried rosemary
- salt to taste

DIRECTIONS

1. Place the potatoes into a large pot with water to cover. Bring to a boil and cook over medium-high heat for about 10 minutes, or until tender.
2. Preheat the grill to medium-high heat. Drain potatoes and toss with olive oil, black pepper, rosemary and salt to taste.
3. Place the potatoes skin-side down over indirect heat on the grill and reserve liquid. Grill for about 15 minutes. Remove potatoes to a serving plate and sprinkle with the reserved olive oil mixture.

HALIBUT WITH RICE WINE

Servings: 6 | Prep: 20m | Cooks: 40m | Total: 1h

NUTRITION FACTS

Calories: 194 | Carbohydrates: 8.6g | Fat: 4.3g | Protein: 23.9g | Cholesterol: 36mg

INGREDIENTS

- 1 teaspoon vegetable oil
- 1 shallots, finely chopped
- 2 cloves garlic, finely chopped
- 1 tablespoon black bean sauce
- 1/2 cup mirin (Japanese sweet wine)
- 1 tablespoon soy sauce
- 1 tablespoon rice vinegar
- 6 (4 ounce) fillets halibut, skin removed
- 1 teaspoon sesame oil
- 1/4 teaspoon pepper
- 2 tablespoons chopped fresh cilantro

DIRECTIONS

1. Heat oil in non-stick saucepan over medium heat. Cook shallots and garlic gently until fragrant, but not brown. Stir in black bean sauce, rice wine, and soy sauce. Bring to boil and cook until reduced by half. Remove from heat, and stir in vinegar; set aside.
2. Pat fish dry. Rub with sesame oil and sprinkle with pepper. Preheat an outdoor grill for high heat, and lightly oil grate.
3. Grill fish for about 5 minutes per side, or just until cooked through. Sprinkle with cilantro. Serve with sauce poured over top.

SAVORY ROASTED ROOT VEGETABLES

Servings: 6 | Prep: 30m | Cooks: 45m | Total: 1h15m

NUTRITION FACTS

Calories: 143 | Carbohydrates: 20.8g | Fat: 4.9g | Protein: 2.8g | Cholesterol: 0mg

INGREDIENTS

- 1 cup diced, raw beet
- 4 carrots, diced
- 2 tablespoons olive oil
- 1 tablespoon dried thyme leaves

- 1 onion, diced
- 2 cups diced potatoes
- 4 cloves garlic, minced
- 1/4 cup canned garbanzo beans (chickpeas), drained
- salt and pepper to taste
- 1/3 cup dry white wine
- 1 cup torn beet greens

DIRECTIONS

1. Preheat an oven to 400 degrees F (200 degrees C).
2. Place the beet, carrot, onion, potatoes, garlic, and garbanzo beans into a 9x13 inch baking dish. Drizzle with the olive oil, then season with thyme, salt, and pepper. Mix well.
3. Bake, uncovered, in the preheated oven for 30 minutes, stirring once midway through baking. Remove the baking dish from the oven, and stir in the wine. Return to the oven, and bake until the wine has mostly evaporated and the vegetables are tender, about 15 minutes more. Stir in the beet greens, allowing them to wilt from the heat of the vegetables. Season to taste with salt and pepper before serving.

HARVARD BEETS

Servings: 3 | Prep: 5m | Cooks: 10m | Total: 15m

NUTRITION FACTS

Calories: 207 | Carbohydrates: 53.1g | Fat: 0g | Protein: 0.1g | Cholesterol: 0mg

INGREDIENTS

- 1 (16 ounce) can beets
- 1/2 cup white vinegar
- 3/4 cup white sugar
- 1 tablespoon cornstarch
- salt to taste

DIRECTIONS

1. Drain the beet liquid into a medium saucepan. To the liquid add vinegar, sugar, cornstarch and salt. Bring to a boil over medium-high heat. Reduce heat to medium; stir in beets and cook until heated through.

CANDIED APPLES

Servings: 15 | Prep: 10m | Cooks: 30m | Total: 40m

NUTRITION FACTS

Calories: 237 | Carbohydrates: 62.5g | Fat: 0.2g | Protein: 0.4g | Cholesterol: 0mg

INGREDIENTS

- 15 apples
- 2 cups white sugar
- 1 cup light corn syrup
- 1 1/2 cups water
- 8 drops red food coloring

DIRECTIONS

1. Lightly grease cookie sheets. Insert craft sticks into whole, stemmed apples.
2. In a medium saucepan over medium-high heat, combine sugar, corn syrup and water. Heat to 300 to 310 degrees F (149 to 154 degrees C), or until a small amount of syrup dropped into cold water forms hard, brittle threads. Remove from heat and stir in food coloring.
3. Holding apple by its stick, dip in syrup and remove and turn to coat evenly. Place on prepared sheets to harden.

ANAHEIM FISH TACOS

Servings: 6 | Prep: 15m | Cooks: 30m | Total: 45m

NUTRITION FACTS

Calories: 273 | Carbohydrates: 29.9g | Fat: 5.1g | Protein: 27.7g | Cholesterol: 36mg

INGREDIENTS

- 1 teaspoon vegetable oil
- 1 Anaheim chile pepper, chopped
- 1 leek, chopped
- 2 cloves garlic, crushed
- salt and pepper to taste
- 1 cup chicken broth
- 2 large tomatoes, diced
- 1/2 teaspoon ground cumin
- 1 1/2 pounds halibut fillets
- 1 lime
- 12 corn tortillas

DIRECTIONS

1. Heat the oil in a large skillet over medium heat, and saute the chile, leek, and garlic until tender and lightly browned. Season with salt and pepper.
2. Mix the chicken broth and tomatoes into the skillet, and season with cumin. Bring to a boil. Reduce heat to low. Place the halibut into the mixture. Sprinkle with lime juice. Cook 15 to 20 minutes until the halibut is easily flaked with a fork. Wrap in warmed corn tortillas to serve.

BEST POTATOES YOU'LL EVER TASTE

Servings: 4 | Prep: 10m | Cooks: 20m | Total: 30m

NUTRITION FACTS

Calories: 283 | Carbohydrates: 47.6g | Fat: 8.5g | Protein: 5.6g | Cholesterol: 4mg

INGREDIENTS

- 3 tablespoons mayonnaise
- 2 cloves garlic, crushed
- 1 teaspoon dried oregano
- salt and pepper to taste
- 5 potatoes, quartered

DIRECTIONS

1. In a small bowl, mix mayonnaise, garlic, oregano, salt , and pepper. Set aside.
2. Bring a large pot of salted water to a boil. Add potatoes, and cook until almost done, about 10 minutes. Don't overcook otherwise the potatoes will break apart. Drain, and cool.
3. Preheat oven broiler. Line a baking tray with aluminum foil, and lightly grease the aluminum foil.
4. Arrange potatoes in the prepared baking tray. Spoon the mayonnaise mixture over the potatoes. Place on the prepared grill, and cook until potatoes are tender and mayonnaise mixture is lightly browned, about 10 minutes.

VEGETARIAN MEATLOAF WITH VEGETABLES

Servings: 9 | Prep: 20m | Cooks: 1h30m | Total: 1h50m

NUTRITION FACTS

Calories: 225 | Carbohydrates: 30.6g | Fat: 4.9g | Protein: 15.1g | Cholesterol: 42mg

INGREDIENTS

- 1/2 (14 ounce) package vegetarian ground beef (e.g., Gimme Lean TM)
- 1 (12 ounce) package vegetarian burger crumbles
- 1 onion, chopped
- 2 eggs, beaten
- 2 tablespoons vegetarian Worcestershire sauce
- 1 teaspoon salt
- 1/3 teaspoon pepper
- 1 teaspoon ground sage
- 1/2 teaspoon garlic powder
- 2 teaspoons prepared mustard
- 1 tablespoon vegetable oil
- 3 1/2 slices bread, cubed
- 1/3 cup milk
- 1 (8 ounce) can tomato sauce
- 4 carrots, cut into 1 inch pieces
- 4 potatoes, cubed
- 1 cooking spray
-

DIRECTIONS

1. Preheat oven to 350 degrees F (175 degrees C).
2. In a large bowl combine vegetarian ground beef, vegetarian ground beef crumbles, onion, eggs, Worcestershire sauce, salt, pepper, sage, garlic powder, mustard, oil, bread cubes and milk. Transfer to a 9 x 13 inch baking dish and form into a loaf. Pour tomato sauce on top.
3. Place carrots and potatoes around loaf and spray vegetables with cooking spray.
4. Bake 30 to 45 minutes; turn vegetables. Bake another 30 to 45 minutes. Let stand 15 minutes before slicing.

BRUSSELS SPROUTS IN MUSTARD SAUCE

Servings: 6 | Prep: 10m | Cooks: 20m | Total: 30m

NUTRITION FACTS

Calories: 41 | Carbohydrates: 9.4g | Fat: 0.4g | Protein: 1.9g | Cholesterol: 0mg

INGREDIENTS

- 2 tablespoons
- 1 pound Brussels sprouts

- cornstarch
- 1/4 cup water
- 1 (14.5 ounce) can chicken broth
- 2 teaspoons prepared Dijon-style mustard
- 2 teaspoons lemon juice

DIRECTIONS

1. Dissolve cornstarch in 1/4 cup water, and set aside.
2. In a medium saucepan over medium heat, bring chicken broth to a boil. Add Brussels sprouts, and cook until tender. Strain, reserving chicken broth, and place Brussels sprouts in a warm serving dish.
3. Return chicken broth to stove, stir in mustard and lemon juice, and return to boil. Add cornstarch mixture. Cook and stir until thickened. Pour over Brussels sprouts to serve.

ORZO WITH KALE

Servings: 10 | Prep: 10m | Cooks: 25m | Total: 35m

NUTRITION FACTS

Calories: 206 | Carbohydrates: 36.1g | Fat: 4.2g | Protein: 7.9g | Cholesterol: 2mg

INGREDIENTS

- 1 teaspoon ground turmeric
- 2 cups uncooked orzo pasta
- 2 tablespoons olive oil
- 4 cloves garlic, sliced
- 1 bunch kale, stems removed and leaves coarsely chopped
- 1 large lemon, juiced
- 1/4 teaspoon ground nutmeg
- 1/4 cup grated Parmesan cheese, or to taste
- salt and black pepper to taste

DIRECTIONS

1. Bring a large pot of lightly-salted water to a boil; sprinkle the turmeric over the boiling water and stir in the orzo; return to a boil. Cook uncovered, stirring occasionally, until the pasta has cooked through, but is still firm to the bite, about 11 minutes; drain. Scrape into a mixing bowl and set aside.

2. Heat the olive oil in a large skillet over medium heat. Cook the garlic in the hot oil for a few seconds until it begins to bubble. Stir the kale into the garlic, cover the skillet with a lid, and cook for 10 minutes. Remove the cover and continue cooking and stirring until the kale is tender, about 10 minutes more. Stir the kale mixture into the orzo along with the lemon juice, nutmeg, and Parmesan cheese. Season with salt and pepper. Serve warm or at room temperature.

LEMON PEPPER PASTA

Servings: 8 | Prep: 5m | Cooks: 15m | Total: 20m

NUTRITION FACTS

Calories: 243 | Carbohydrates: 43g | Fat: 4.2g | Protein: 7.5g | Cholesterol: 0mg

INGREDIENTS

- 1 pound spaghetti
- 2 tablespoons olive oil
- 3 tablespoons lemon juice, to taste
- 1 tablespoon dried basil
- ground black pepper to taste

DIRECTIONS

1. Bring a large pot of lightly salted water to a boil. Add pasta and cook for 8 to 10 minutes, or until done; drain.
2. In a small bowl, combine olive oil, lemon juice, basil and black pepper. Mix well and toss with the pasta. Serve hot or cold.

PORK CHOP AND CABBAGE CASSEROLE

Servings: 4 | Prep: 30m | Cooks: 1h30m | Total: 2h

NUTRITION FACTS

Calories: 370 | Carbohydrates: 54.2g | Fat: 8.3g | Protein: 21.5g | Cholesterol: 42mg

INGREDIENTS

- 1 small head cabbage, shredded
- 4 potatoes, peeled and sliced
- 1/2 (10.75 ounce) can water
- 1 small onion, diced

- salt to taste
- 1 (10.75 ounce) can condensed cream of chicken soup
- 4 pork chops

DIRECTIONS

1. Preheat oven to 350 degrees F (175 degrees C). Lightly grease a 9x13 baking dish.
2. Place a layer of shredded cabbage into baking dish and then a layer of sliced potatoes. Repeat cabbage and potatoes and salt.
3. Simmer the soup, water and diced onion. Pour over cabbage and potatoes.
4. In a skillet, brown each pork chop in a small amount of oil and place on top of mixture. Bake for 1 1/2 hours uncovered or until chops are tender.

SPANISH RICE

Servings: 6 | Prep: 20m | Cooks: 40m | Total: 1h

NUTRITION FACTS

Calories: 269 | Carbohydrates: 54.8g | Fat: 2.9g | Protein: 5.2g | Cholesterol: 0mg

INGREDIENTS

- 1 tablespoon vegetable oil
- 2 cups uncooked long-grain white rice
- 1/4 onion, chopped
- 1 green bell pepper, chopped
- salt and pepper to taste
- 1 (14.5 ounce) can stewed tomatoes
- 4 cups water

DIRECTIONS

1. In a large skillet, combine oil, rice, onion, green pepper and salt and pepper until the rice is a light brown color. Remove skillet from stove.
2. Mix tomatoes into the mixture. Pour in water (it should cover the entire mixture; use more if necessary). Return the skillet to the stovetop and bring the mixture to a full boil; salt and pepper to taste. When the mixture begins to boil, cover the skillet, and reduce heat to a simmer. Cook 12 to 15 minutes and never, I mean NEVER, remove the cover. After 12 to 15 minutes, turn stove off and let stand for another 12 to 15 minutes. DO NOT remove cover until the final 15 minutes has elapsed!

BARLEY AND MUSHROOMS WITH BEANS

Servings: 6 | Prep: 15p | Cooks: 1h | Total: 1h15m

NUTRITION FACTS

Calories: 202 | Carbohydrates: 39g | Fat: 2.1g | Protein: 9.1g | Cholesterol: 0mg

INGREDIENTS

- 1 teaspoon olive oil
- 3 cups sliced fresh mushrooms
- 1 cup chopped onion
- 1/2 cup chopped celery
- 2 cloves garlic, minced
- 1/2 cup uncooked barley
- 3 cups vegetable broth
- 1 (15.5 ounce) can white beans, drained

DIRECTIONS

1. Heat oil in a medium saucepan over medium heat, and stir in mushrooms, onion, celery, and garlic. Saute until tender.
2. Mix barley and vegetable broth into the saucepan. Bring to a boil, cover, and reduce heat. Simmer 45 to 50 minutes, until barley is tender.
3. Stir white beans into the barley mixture. Continue cooking about 5 minutes, until beans are heated.

LEMON ASPARAGUS RISOTTO

Servings: 4 | Prep: 15m | Cooks: 45m | Total: 1h

NUTRITION FACTS

Calories: 357 | Carbohydrates: 53.4g | Fat: 8.7g | Protein: 11.1g | Cholesterol: 8mg

INGREDIENTS

- 20 fresh asparagus spears, trimmed
- 4 cups low-sodium chicken broth
- 2 tablespoons olive oil
- 1 small onion, diced
- 1 stalk celery, diced
- 1 clove garlic, minced
- 1 cup arborio rice
- 1/2 cup dry white wine
- 1/4 cup freshly grated Parmesan cheese
- 2 tablespoons lemon juice

- 1/4 teaspoon salt
- 1/4 teaspoon ground black pepper
- 1/2 teaspoon lemon zest

DIRECTIONS

1. Place a steamer insert into a saucepan and fill with water to just below the bottom of the steamer. Bring water to a boil. Add asparagus, cover, and steam until tender, about 5 minutes. Cut asparagus into 1-inch pieces; set aside.
2. Heat chicken broth in a saucepan over medium heat; keep at a simmer while preparing risotto.
3. Heat olive oil in a large skillet over medium heat. Cook and stir onion and celery until vegetables are tender, about 5 minutes. Season with salt and black pepper. Stir in garlic and arborio rice; cook and stir until rice is lightly toasted, about 5 more minutes.
4. Pour white wine into rice mixture, stirring constantly, until liquid is evaporated, about 5 minutes. Stir chicken broth into rice, one ladleful at a time, allowing liquid to absorb completely before adding more while stirring constantly, about 20 minutes. Add asparagus and stir.
5. Remove from heat and mix in Parmesan cheese, lemon juice and lemon zest. Serve immediately.

VEGETARIAN REFRIED BEANS

Servings: 12 | Prep: 15m | Cooks: 4h15m | Total: 4h30m

NUTRITION FACTS

Calories: 161 | Carbohydrates: 25.3g | Fat: 3.1g | Protein: 8.5g | Cholesterol: 0mg

INGREDIENTS

- 1 pound dry pinto beans, rinsed
- 2 tablespoons minced garlic, divided
- 1 medium tomato, diced
- 2 tablespoons ground cumin
- 1 tablespoon chili powder
- 2 tablespoons olive oil
- salt to taste

DIRECTIONS

1. Place the beans in a large saucepan, and cover with an inch of water. Place over high heat, and bring to a boil. When the beans have come to a boil, drain, and return them to the same pot. Cover the beans with 2 inches of water, and stir in 1 tablespoon of garlic, the tomato, cumin, and chili powder. Bring to a boil over high heat, then reduce heat to low, and simmer until the beans are very soft, about 3 hours and 45 minutes, adding water as needed.

2. Once the beans have cooked, mash them with the remaining tablespoon of garlic, the oil, and salt to taste; use additional water as needed to achieve desired consistency. Place over low heat for 30 minutes, stirring occasionally. Serve.

VEGETARIAN LIME ORZO

Servings: 4 | Prep: 35m | Cooks: 17m | Total: 52m

NUTRITION FACTS

Calories: 535 | Carbohydrates: 87.4g | Fat: 12.3g | Protein: 20.9g | Cholesterol: 11mg

INGREDIENTS

- 2 tablespoons olive oil
- 2 cloves garlic, minced
- 2 cups orzo pasta
- 1 zucchini, peeled and shredded
- 1 carrot, peeled and shredded
- 1 (16 ounce) can stewed tomatoes, undrained
- 1 (14 ounce) can vegetable broth
- 1 teaspoon Italian seasoning
- 1 teaspoon dried basil leaves
- salt and black pepper to taste
- 1/4 cup chopped green onions
- 1/4 cup chopped fresh parsley
- 2 teaspoons grated lime zest
- 2 tablespoons lime juice
- 1/2 cup grated Parmesan cheese for topping

DIRECTIONS

1. Heat the olive oil in a large skillet over medium-high heat. Stir in the garlic and orzo pasta; cook and stir until pasta turns a light, golden color, about 5 minutes. Stir in zucchini and carrots; cook until vegetables soften, about 2 minutes. Stir in the tomatoes, vegetable broth, Italian seasoning, and basil. Season with salt and pepper to taste. Reduce heat to medium. Cover, and simmer until almost all liquid is absorbed, about 10 minutes. Stir in the green onions, parsley, lime zest, and lime juice. Remove from heat, cool slightly, and serve sprinkled with Parmesan cheese.

Printed in Great Britain
by Amazon

48198196R00075